CHILD OF LUST

CHILD OF LUST

"Tears are words that need to be written." —Paulo Coelho

TONY STCYR

LIBERTY HILL PUBLISHING

Liberty Hill Publishing
2301 Lucien Way #415
Maitland, FL 32751
407.339.4217
www.libertyhillpublishing.com

Paperback ISBN-13: 978-1-66286-563-3
Ebook ISBN-13: 978-1-66286-565-7

This Book Is Dedicated to James & James

James Richter – There truly is a "friend that sticketh closer than a brother," and you, James Richter, are that friend. Without your help, inspiration, and spiritual guidance over the past three decades, I just don't know where I would be today. You have been more than a mentor; you have been a true help during my times of need. When I felt the need to write this book, you were there, helping me through the writing and editing process. If there are any grammatical errors in the book, I can blame you (humor). Thank you so much!

James "Butch" Allen – You already know how I feel about you, cuz. Being there for me when no one else was is a credit to the godly man you are. Your assistance in providing stories, information, and photos for this book were a tremendous help in answering my questions and filling in empty spaces in my life. Thanks for always being there. Without you, this book would never have been written. And without your care, concern, and godly example, I would not be the man I am today.

TABLE OF CONTENTS

PREFACE

It has taken much courage for me to allow millions of people inside my secret place, a place where I very seldom ventured and tried to avoid over the past forty-plus years. You are about to embark on a journey into some dark areas that may be hard to believe for some while possibly being offensive to others. Either way, you are about to experience a rollercoaster ride of emotions.

I am pleased that you have chosen to experience this journey I have lived. It is my prayer that this story of a scared, abused, neglected, and abandoned little boy and his family experiences will help others who have gone through or may be going through some of the same challenges today. I also feel it's necessary for my children and grandchildren and people who know me to understand how my childhood experiences have shaped me into the man I am today (both good and bad), and why I respond the way I do to isolation and rejection. Stories and quotes in this book are not meant to offend, degrade or assassinate anyone's character but only to allow the reader to experience the feelings and emotions that I have experienced most of my life.

I do not use profanity, nor do I condone the use of profanity. However, to help the reader understand and feel the true sentiments of a few characters, at the advice of the publisher and the editor, it was suggested that since the profane words were mild and would have a PG rating, the exact words are used in place of $#?%.

It is my prayer that every reader who has been through abuse, neglect, or abandonment can take solace in my story and apply hope to their lives. It is also my hope that every expectant mother who is faced with a difficult decision will understand the lifelong and generational consequences that her decision will have and be inspired to make the correct choice.

May God touch and bless each person who reads my story.

Child of Lust is based on true characters and true-life events.
In certain case and events, characters, and timelines may have been
dramatized or filled in due to exact details being lost or forgotten over
the years or not fully remembered by relatives who contributed.
A great big thank you to all of you who assisted during the information-gathering process.

CHAPTER I

THE WHISTLING BABY

It was Friday. A light rain was falling on that cool, colorful October evening as Tony turned into the empty parking lot of Mowell Funeral Home in Fayetteville, Georgia. Tony and his wife Donnie were the first to arrive for Marilyn's early viewing.

"What time is it?" Tony asked as he pulled his silver Ram pickup into a front parking space.

Donnie looked at her husband's arm and saw his watch stuck out from under his sport coat sleeve, then she glanced at the clock on the dash that was in plain view. Donnie knew her husband's emotions had been a mess since Marilyn died on Wednesday, so she looked at her watch and replied, "Four-thirty."

Tony put the vehicle in park, tapped his apple watch, looked at the time, and said, "We're early."

He looked at Donnie, who was texting, and asked, "The family knows we're supposed to be here by 5 o'clock, don't they?"

Without looking up, Donnie replied, "Yes, I notified everyone."

Tony turned and began to look out the driver side window at the funeral home, remembering the last time he was here.

"It was just a few years ago when I preached at Alice's funeral," Tony said in a soft, faint voice.

Donnie didn't respond, she just kept texting. Tony wasn't really waiting for a response; he was just thinking aloud. He turned and saw his wife still texting, then looked back toward the chapel area and began to think about Alice.

In many ways Alice had been like a second mom to Tony. He lived with her on and off when he was growing up. After an abusive relationship with her first husband, she divorced and remained single for several years. Since she didn't have any kids, she spent a lot of time and money spoiling her nieces and nephews. She was known for being the "go-to" aunt when anyone in the family needed a place to stay or a little spending money. She was always willing to help where she could.

When Alice met Bob House, it was love at first sight. Bob was a divorcee with three children. When Alice married Bob, it was a match made in heaven. Alice loved children and was very accepting of Bob's children, which made Bob incredibly happy. Bob worked at the Ford plant in Hapeville, where he made good money, and that also made Alice happy since she never had much and loved security. You could tell Bob and Alice were perfect for each other since they got along great and rarely had any disagreements.

Not long after they were married, Alice gave birth to a healthy baby boy they named Richard, but they called him Ricky for short. Less than three years later, they had a second son they named Jonathan but called him Johnny. Since Alice and Bob now had two children and Bob's older children lived with them part-time, he decided they needed a larger home, so he bought a new house on Yarmouth Drive in Jonesboro. It wasn't much bigger than the house in Hapeville, but it had two much-needed bathrooms.

As Tony got to know Bob, they became close, and his new mild-mannered uncle became a father figure to him. Bob took Tony fishing, hunting, and did things with him his dad never did. Both Bob and Alice treated Tony as if he were their own son, and he loved it. When Tony started driving, he was able to spend a lot more time at Alice and Bob's house. He loved doing things with Ricky and Johnny, and he especially enjoyed teaching Ricky how to play baseball.

When Ricky was eight, Tony was teaching him how to catch fly balls in their backyard. Tony was tossing a baseball up in the air about ten feet above Ricky, and he was catching each fly ball without any difficulty. After seeing how easy Ricky was catching them, Tony decided to toss one a little higher. Tony was planning to throw the ball only about twenty feet into the air, but he threw the ball much farther than he had anticipated straight over Ricky's head. Ricky was tracking the ball with his glove turned up over his face, watching and waiting for the ball to drop in it. But it didn't. The ball missed his glove, hit Ricky in the forehead, bounced straight up, and dropped to the ground. Tony's first response was to laugh, but then he thought he may be severely injured.

"Are you okay?" Tony asked frantically as he grabbed Ricky and closely inspected his forehead.

Ricky had thrown his glove to the ground and was rubbing his forehead with both hands, "I . . . I . . . think so . . . yeah, I'm good," Ricky hesitantly replied.

"No blood, no broken skin. You look ok," Tony responded, "but I still think we should call it a day."

Tony breathed a sigh of relief as they headed to the house. He checked Ricky's head again and laughed, "It's a good thing you've got a hard head!" Ricky looked up at his older cousin with disdain and said, "You need to learn how to pitch!"

Since Tony was staying a lot at Alice and Bob's, helping Ricky and Johnny's stepsister Pam babysit, and staying nearly every weekend, helping Bob work on an old TV, CB radio, car, or motorcycle, he finally asked if he could move in with them, and they agreed. Just before Tony's seventeenth birthday, he happily left Blair Village Apartments, the government projects he and his mom moved into when they left Kennesaw, and moved in with Alice and Bob. He lived with them until he married Donnie four years later.

"That's funny!" Tony whispered out loud to no one in particular.

Donnie looked up from her phone with a puzzled look and asked, "What's funny?"

Tony turned and replied, "I was thinking about Ricky and the time I threw the baseball up, and it fell and hit him square in the forehead."

"I remember you telling me that story," Donnie replied. "What made you think of that?"

"I was thinking about Alice, and I thought of Ricky, and that story came to mind," Tony paused, smiling, and said, "I'm glad it did . . . I needed a good laugh." He then turned his attention back to the funeral home.

Donnie dropped the conversation. She knew her husband often thought of memories from his past, both happy and sad, so she went back to her texting.

"This is a nice funeral home," Tony whispered as he reached and turned off the ignition. "Possibly the nicest I've ever seen."

The funeral home is picturesque. There are twelve sixteen-foot-high white columns spaced ten feet apart around the spacious front porch. There are six columns in the front and six columns perfectly aligned to the rear. The funeral home is constructed of light-colored brick with brown shading, which caused the large columns to captivate you as you pull into the entrance. Extending beyond the porch to the left are the administrative offices and family conference rooms. To the right of the porch is the chapel and the funeral procession parking area. The shrubs and hedges are immaculately shaped and trimmed, and the windows and shutters are bright and inviting. Chandeliers can be seen through the upper transom windows, which further add to the bright and beautiful appearance. There are no steps to navigate, which makes it easy for anyone to enter through the wood and glass French doors that are perfectly positioned in the center of the veranda.

As Tony admired the brilliant structure, Donnie was checking on how far away their children were and making sure they had not been delayed by traffic or the rain.

"Rachel is going to be late," Donnie announced, still looking at her phone.

Tony turned to her and said, "I don't care, as long as she's here. Did she get with Leah about singing during the service tomorrow?"

"She did," Donnie said assuredly. "They're supposed to get with you about which songs to sing, though."

Rachel is Tony and Donnie's oldest child. She has always been the social butterfly of the family, being she never meets a stranger. She grew up a loving and caring person, which many of her family and friends either take advantage of or criticize her for. She has her dad's personality and her mom's good looks. When Rachel was a teenager, she and Donnie were mistaken several times as sisters. Rachel has naturally black hair, but now that she's older, she colors her hair brown, red, or black, depending on her mood. Rachel is five-foot-nine, wears glasses, and is still thin after giving birth to four children. She's been singing on stage since she was nine and was the lead singer of the family's gospel group from 1990 until they disbanded in 2014.

Rachel's social interaction started when she was about two years old. She would approach complete strangers and introduce herself by saying, "I'm Rachel. What's your name?" Although Tony and Donnie were happy their daughter was friendly, this concerned them, so whenever they went to a park, store, or the mall, they would put a harness on Rachel and strap the lead to their hand or stroller. People have accused them of being abusive or treating her like a dog, but because of her willingness to run to strangers and talk to anyone anywhere, they felt this was the safest way to keep her from being abducted. It obviously worked.

Rachel was a beautiful baby. She was also very talented as a young child. When she was nine months old, a business owner offered to sponsor her in a beauty contest. She entered and placed second out of thirty entries. Tony believed she would have finished first if he had not botched the entrance form, the section marked "Favorite Foods." Tony figured she was too young to know what her favorite foods were, so he left that section blank. It was only when the announcer started saying, "bananas, carrots," and other baby food flavors when talking about favorite foods of the other contestants that Tony realized what the judges were asking for. But he figures finishing second with a blank section is as good as a first-place finish. Since Tony and Donnie caught some flak from people at church for entering her into a beauty contest, they decided not to enter her anymore even though they felt she could have made the cover of some baby magazines.

When Rachel was eighteen months old, her sister Leah was born. Shortly after coming home from the hospital, Donnie learned that Rachel had acquired a rare and unique talent not many, if any, her age acquire. Donnie was in the kitchen preparing dinner one afternoon when she heard a loud and distinct whistle. The sound clearly came from inside the house, which nearly scared Donnie to death. She knew Tony was at work, so it wasn't him. She then looked in the living room and saw the baby sleeping in the bassinette and knew she didn't make the sound. She knew Rachel was in her bedroom playing and thought, *Surely it's not her*. While she was trying to figure out where the whistling came from, she heard it again. The concerned mother stepped into the living room and looked down the hallway, trying to figure out who or what was making the whistle sound. When she heard it the third time, she realized it came from Rachel's bedroom.

Tony must have gotten her a new toy that whistles, she thought. But not knowing for certain, she called out, "Rachel, come to Mommy."

As Rachel stepped into the hall, she saw her one-year-old poke her lips out and whistle. Knowing her husband would have a tough time believing their daughter whistles, she kept Rachel whistling until he got home. Donnie had Rachel whistle several times for her dad. The young couple were both excited and fascinated with their toddler's newfound talent. For weeks, Rachel whistled for family, friends, and even strangers at stores and restaurants.

"A baby that whistles," people would say with admiration.

Tony would proudly reply, "She's not even potty trained yet, but she can whistle!"

Rachel was a star! If social media had been around then, the "Whistling Baby" may have gone viral. But after everyone had seen her whistle and months passed without her parents making her whistle, Rachel forgot how, and things returned to normal for the little star. This disappointed Tony, but at least he was able to get her whistling on an old film reel.

Rachel was quite the little salesperson too. At five years old, her parents enrolled her into kindergarten at Faith Christian Academy in Fayetteville, Georgia. Since FCA was a Christian school, every class had to sell candy bars to raise money to cover school expenses. Her kindergarten year, she outsold her entire school and won the top cash prize. She received enough money to buy her a new bicycle. When the church sold donuts to raise money for their building fund, Rachel was the top seller. She was so adorable hardly anyone could say no to her.

Before she was ten, she was having intelligent conversations with teenagers as well as adults. Her vocabulary was amazing for her early age, and her ability to articulate with older people surprised many.

When she was in the fourth grade, she sang a song her dad wrote about child abuse called, "Please Don't Hurt Me, Mr. Man" in her school's talent contest. She brought the judges and faculty to tears. Her voice was amazing for such a young child, and she had no stage fright whatsoever.

By the time Rachel was twelve, she knew what she wanted in life. She would tell anyone who would listen that when she grew up, she wanted to get married and have a house full of kids. Becoming a wife and a mother is all she talked about. Although she dreamed of having a large family, Rachel didn't get married to her husband Jonathan Lucas until she was twenty-seven, and by then, many of her childbearing years had escaped her. But after eight pregnancies, four which were miscarriages, she and her husband are the proud parents of four healthy and energetic children. Although Rachel considers her firstborn daughter Somerlyn to be her "miracle" baby, as much trouble as she had bearing children, Tony told her the other three boys are miracles as well.

Rachel and her family lived in Jackson, Georgia, for several years, only a few miles from her parents, so Tony and Donnie got to visit with them regularly. But in July 2017, Jonathan's dad had a health scare, so Jonathan moved the family to Falcon, North Carolina, where he was from, so he could be close to his dad. They still live in Falcon, North Carolina, today, which is over a seven-hour drive from Tony and Donnie since they live in Adairsville, Georgia, now. But Tony and Donnie are hoping they will move back to Georgia soon so they can be closer to their grandchildren . . . and Rachel and Jonathan.

Tony looked at his wife as she put her phone in her purse and asked, "You ready to go in?"

Donnie laid her hand on Tony's arm, looked him in the eyes, and asked, "Are you?"

Tony wasn't sure how to answer. He didn't really know the answer. He looked back out the window, looked down at the seat, then looked at his wife, and said softly, "I don't know."

Donnie sat silent as she watched her grief-stricken husband wrestle with his emotions. Tony looked back out the front windshield and into the grayness as the raindrops fell like light tears on the glass before him. Then he unfastened his seat belt, opened his door, and said, "I'm ready!"

Bob, Alice and Ricky House.

Rachel singing at Kemp Elementary.

Rachel with her award for singing, "Please Don't Hurt Me Mr. Man".

CHAPTER II

SHINY DOORKNOBS

"Funeral homes have that distinct . . . smell, don't they?" Tony spoke to his faithful wife as they stood in the lobby, brushing rain droplets off their clothes.

"I believe it's the smell of the flowers," Donnie replied. "I should've brought my umbrella in; it may be raining harder when we leave tonight."

Tony didn't answer. He was focused on the closed double doors near the end of the hall on the right where a ring of light from a wall-mounted lamp illuminated the guest register.

A funeral associate emerged from his office, approached the couple, and said, "Welcome! You must be here for Marilyn's early viewing."

"Looks like we're the first," Tony responded. "But there should be a few more here by 5:00, some even later."

"That'll be fine," the funeral associate said as he handed Tony and Donnie a memorial program.

Tony looked at the picture of Marilyn on the front and smiled," This is a great picture of her."

"It is," Donnie affirmed.

Tony looked it over, front to back. Even though he had approved a proof earlier that morning, he wanted to make sure the information he provided was accurate.

"Look's good!" Tony told the associate. "You guys did a wonderful job." He folded the program, then slipped it into the inside pocket of his sport coat. He looked back down the hall toward the double doors and asked, "Is that Marilyn's room?"

The associate replied, "Yes. And since there are no other funerals scheduled this weekend, we have her in the room that accesses the chapel. The door to the chapel is open, and ya'll are welcome to sit in there if you'd like. I'll start the video on the big screen whenever you're ready, and you can practice with the piano if you need to."

"Thank you so much!" Tony and Donnie both shared their gratitude for the kindness extended to them by the funeral home.

"You're welcome." As the associate turned to leave, he said, "Let us know when everyone arrives. Bryan will open the doors once the rest of the family is here."

Tony and Donnie thanked the associate again and then proceeded down the hall toward the viewing room. As they reached the registry station, Tony stood, silently staring at the closed doors while his wife wrote both their names in the registry book.

Donnie looked at her husband, who was focused on the parlor doors. "I don't believe I've ever been the first person to write in a guest book." Donnie was trying to get a response from Tony who was still focused on the parlor doors. He stood silent, dreading the events that lay beyond the shiny doorknobs.

Tony's natural grey hair mingled with his fading black locks made him look like a distinguished gentleman of sorts. His nicely trimmed salt and peppered goatee enhances his already handsome appearance and hides the two scars on the left side of his face. When Tony first grew his goatee, Donnie told him she didn't like it. She also told him it made him look older, but that was contrary to what other people told him. Many of their friends, mostly women, told him it made him look younger, and that may be why Donnie didn't like it. But when Tony explained that it keeps him from shaving every day and hides his scars, she accepted it and later began to like it.

Tony had a golf ball size patch of grey hair appear on the left side of his head when he was eight, so he's been used to having grey hair for a long time. At school and family events, his little grey patch was quite the conversation starter. It made him feel special and different, not the special and different that came from being poor, abused, and neglected—he knew that special and different—but the special and different feeling one might experience as a celebrity. It came when people paid attention to him and pointed out something pleasant in his life instead of the vulgar names he was used to hearing at home. He especially loved it when his teachers would fawn over him. It made his classmates jealous and sometimes angry at him, but he felt like that was a positive because at least he was being noticed and not ignored. Everywhere he went, children and grownups would come up to him and say, "You have paint in your hair!" Tony would light up with excitement that someone spoke to him without using profanity or harsh language. He would then explain how the patch just appeared when he was eight, and two of his aunts had grey hair when they were young. Being noticed helped him through some emotionally tough times.

He was proud of his grey hair as a child and is thankful for it today. He often jokes that he didn't care what color his hair turned as long as it didn't turn loose. Other than a small receding hairline, his wish has come true. And since early greying happened to a couple of his children, he considers grey hair hereditary and not a sign of old age.

His silver rim glasses rest comfortably on his nose and makes his dark brown eyes seem soft and friendly. His left eye, which is a lazy eye, sometimes winks when he smiles. He looks fifteen years younger than his ripe old age of sixty. He stands six feet tall and is a little pudgy around the waist, but the brown tweed sports coat he's wearing atop his dark brown slacks and light blue shirt hides the extra pounds well.

Tony was normally the life of the party, the one who's cracking jokes, making witty comments, and causing others to smile. But tonight, he's not smiling. He's not talking much either. He's in deep thought, grieving, and wrestling with feelings he's never felt before. Trying to make sense of his past, Marilyn's past, so many unanswered questions, lies, hidden dark secrets, and scars beneath the surface not easily hidden like the ones on his face, all these things weighed heavy on his mind as he stands facing the white wooden doors leading to Marilyn's final memorial service. The rest of the family would arrive soon. But for now, Tony isn't thinking about the arriving family, he wants answers he's been seeking for years. And now that Marilyn's gone, there's only one person left who can give him those answers . . . Butch!

Four-year-old Tony dressed like a hobo holding first-place Dr. Kildare kit.

Tony sporting his grey patch.

CHAPTER III

No Peace for the Peacemaker

The funeral associate paced back and forth in front of the entry way focusing on the parking lot as he glances at his watch every few minutes, looking at the rain-soaked white striped asphalt, watching as more early visitors begin pulling into the closest available parking spaces. Among them are three of Tony and Donnie's grown children, three of his grandchildren, his cousin Sandra, her husband, and the minister and his wife. The funeral director holds the door open and smiles as he greets each rain-sprinkled guest, takes their umbrellas, and hands them a memorial announcement.

Hearing the familiar voices of family members brought Tony back from the skeletons in his mind. He stepped away from the parlor doors and is now standing by Donnie as the early visitors make their way down the hallway toward them.

Donnie greets everyone with a hug and encourages them to sign the registry book. Donnie's efficient like that. It's her personality to be detailed. Her once tall and thin frame has also put on a few pounds over the forty years she and Tony have been married. Tony often jokes by telling her that they need to renew their wedding vows because there's an extra hundred pounds on her that he didn't say, "I do" to. She would respond by poking him in the belly and saying, "What about yourself?" After forty years of marriage, she's used to his playful comments, although when he says things like that in public, it bothers her a little.

Being that her dad was a holiness preacher, Donnie still lives by most of her dad's teachings. She still has long hair at age fifty-eight, which is a beautiful mix of gray and black that flows down her back and to her knees. She still wears modest apparel and no slacks, shorts, or short dresses. She does wear a wedding ring and a Pandora necklace with a matching bracelet Tony bought her, but she doesn't wear earrings or other jewelry, something her dad was completely against. She still wears a headband or clip-on hair bows to keep her long hair from falling into her face. But tonight, her hair is hanging naturally.

Tony likes her to leave it down. "You have such pretty hair; you should let it hang down more." Tony says that to her quite often. When she's in public and at work, she gets a lot of compliments on her long hair. The natural look of gray and black mix is a frosted color that many women pay hundreds of dollars for. But Donnie's is all-natural with no dyes or coloring, just raw beauty. Other than trimming it once a few years ago, she hasn't cut it since she was seventeen years old.

While standing in the hallway, Tony and Donnie got a few consoling hugs from the minister and his wife, their youngest son Caleb, and a few others. When his youngest daughter approached, she gave her dad a cold, half-hearted hug from the side. Tony hugged her back as they exchanged a few pleasantries, and then she moved on to converse with the other guests.

His relationship with her over the past few years has been estranged, to say the least. She went for more than two years without calling Tony or her mom; not on Father's Day, Mother's Day, Christmas, birthdays, nothing. She had once been an advocate for the family staying close, in touch, but something changed. Tony felt like it was because of a business arrangement he had with her and Sam that went south, which caused a lot of finger pointing and a huge dispute over who was responsible for a $110,000.00 loan. Tony eventually assumed the loan and paid most of it off, but to this day, Tony nor anyone in the family can figure out what caused such a division in the family, especially after they had all been so close.

When the shunning began, Tony told her and Sam that they had good reason to mistreat him, but they shouldn't mistreat their mother since she didn't have anything to do with the partnership or the loan. Although Sam and Leah were giving both their parents the silent treatment, Tony knew their main target was him. He knew he should've handled things differently. He told Leah during this time that he was dead to her, and he regrets ever making that comment. He knows now it was his head talking and not his heart, but that was the way he felt at the time. He also knows he didn't handle the business partnership with Sam and his wife like he should've, and he cried many tears over the incident, but he still didn't feel like his actions rose to the level of having his relationship with them severed. They had disagreements in the past and had always worked through them, so Tony was hoping they could work through this one as well.

Tony loved his children and poured his entire young adult life into them, making certain they would have a much better childhood than he did, a stable home free from drugs and alcohol and a bright future once they became adults. He knew he wasn't the perfect father, but he wasn't striving for perfection since he didn't know what a "perfect father" was, he just wanted to be . . . in their lives. He never knew what that was like growing up, but he did know what not having a father in his life was like, so he worked hard making sure his children didn't experience that.

Without all his children in his life, he was miserable, sad, and isolated. It was his childhood re-emerging. The feelings of loneliness, rejection, and abandonment all came rushing in again. And although Tony kept reaching out to them for two long years, they didn't seem as interested in making amends as quickly as he was. But finally, Tony's persistency paid off, and about a year ago, they met and started making progress to rebuild their relationship. And though the relationship with Sam has improved greatly, the jury is still out on whether Leah is ready to forgive, forget, and move forward.

When Sam and his family approached, Tony lit up. He had not seen his grandkids since the previous Christmas. He squeezed each one with excitement as he complimented them on how tall they had grown since he last saw them. He kept squeezing and hugging them until he finally released them to go hug their Nana. That's what they call Donnie. He hugged his daughter-in-law, and when he turned around, he paused for a moment, then Sam reached out and gave his dad a big bear hug. They held each other for close to a minute as they kept saying how much they loved and missed each other. Tony was crying, something he doesn't do often. He wasn't sure if it was from seeing Sam and his family again or from the emotions he had been holding in since Marilyn's death. Whichever it was, it felt good, and Tony was going to enjoy every moment.

Sam towered over his dad at six-foot-nine and a firm but slender 240 pounds. He's always been the apple of Tony's eye and, because of that, he was spoiled a lot growing up. He did carry his share of the whippings since he was a bit mischievous and would often be mean to his sisters, but if you asked him if he was spoiled, he'll smile, curl his lips upward, poke them out, and nod his head yes, which is usually followed by a burst of laughter.

He is known by many in the family as "The Gentle Giant." Tony's aunt Doris on his dad's side gave him that name when he was a teenager. Sam always dresses nice and neat, keeps a tight haircut, and is friendly to everyone he meets. He has a soft laid-back nature, but if you push him too far, he could unleash all six-foot-nine inches and 240 pounds on you without batting an eye, although no one has ever seen him that upset.

When Sam drew away from Tony, it really hurt. Tony believes Sam hurt just as much as he did during the silent treatment. Although Tony can't prove it, he believes someone was encouraging him to pull away from his parents. Tony just can't accept the fact that Sam would do his dad and mom that way without some sort of outside influence. He's too good a person and too much of a loving son.

When they released, Sam looked at his dad and asked, "You doin' okay?"

"Yeah, I suppose, considering . . ." Tony sighed, then deflected the conversation away from himself. "How about you?"

"Working all the time," Sam replied. "Between People's Janitorial and my lawncare business, I stay pretty busy."

While Sam was growing up, he and Tony were as close as a father and son could be. He was his firstborn son, the first grandson, and up until Caleb was born ten years later, he was the only hope of carrying on the StCyr family name.

Ever since Sam was old enough to hold a plastic bat, Tony was in the yard playing catch or teaching him how to hit or pitch. Tony would hurry home from work just so he and Sam could play ball in the yard before supper. Tony even had a streetlight installed so they could play after dark. The girls would play sometimes, but Sam always wanted to hit and throw with his dad as soon as he got home. And it didn't matter whose birthday it was, there was always a ball game in the front yard before and after cake.

One such birthday party took place when Sam was twelve. The front yard was full of children playing whiffle ball when some boys came riding by the house on their bicycles, shouting absurd comments and making rude gestures toward Tony's children and the birthday guests. They kept riding past the house into the circle, then turning around and riding back by the house, shouting the lewd comments. Tony had never seen these boys on Price Drive West before, so he knew they had to be from another neighborhood.

After a few more passes, Tony had enough. He was standing on the front porch watching when the boys entered the circle. He took off running as fast as he could across the large front yard, running uphill toward the street where the group of eight riders who looked to be ten to twelve years in age was circling. When the boys saw Tony coming, they started pedaling faster to keep from being caught, but one boy wasn't fast enough. Tony grabbed the handlebars of his bicycle, stepped in front of the bike, and after catching his breath, asked him angrily, "Why are you and your friends harassing these kids!"

"We . . . were . . . ju . . . just . . . having a little fun, that's all," the boy responded timidly with a lot less arrogance than he had shown just a minute earlier.

The other boys had stopped down the street and were watching to see what was going to happen to their friend.

"I tell you what," Tony responded, "If you want to have some fun, you go tell your friends to come back and have some cake and ice cream and play some whiffle ball with the rest of the kids."

The boy looked shocked and said surprisingly, "Okay, I'll ask them."

Tony turned loose of the handlebars and started back toward the house, still winded from where he had sprinted uphill across the large yard. *Whew, I can't be doing that anymore!* Tony thought as he was taking long deep breaths, walking slowly down the gravel drive.

A few minutes later, the boys came riding up to the yard, dropped their bicycles in the ditch at the edge of the street, and slowly walked into the yard. Tony called out to them and motioned for them to come on down and meet the other kids who had stopped playing ball and were now watching with great anticipation as the boys approached them. After some apologies, introduction, and handshakes, the kids picked teams and started playing whiffle ball together. No lude jesters and no name-calling, just a bunch of kids who were at odds with each other a few minutes ago now laughing, making friends, and having a good time.

Tony brought cake and ice cream to each of the new arrivals and handed each one a drink. After an hour, one of the boys' parents drove up looking for their son. Tony met them at the edge of the street and invited them to come have some refreshments with the rest of the party guests. Tony explained that he had invited the boys to join in the festivities but didn't say anything about their rude behavior. The parents explained that their son had to leave due to a previous commitment, so they told their son to hurry home and then drove off. After a few minutes, all the boys said their goodbyes, mounted their bikes, and headed down the street, popping wheelies and waving as they left. Tony had just walked up on to the porch and was standing by Donnie as the boys rode off. Tony was thinking about the day's events and how they had unfolded. He was hoping this birthday party and the lessons learned would be remembered and cherished not only by his family but everyone involved, including the mystery boys.

"You old softy!" Donnie said to her husband with a look of pride and admiration.

Tony looked at his wife surprisingly. "What do you mean by that?"

As Donnie watched the boys disappear down the street, she said, "That was amazing what you did; how you turned that situation around."

"I guess it was," Tony smiled. "The Bible says, 'overcome evil with good.' I just figured the way they were acting, they were jealous of the fun our kids were having, and their response was to be ugly and attack them."

Donnie thought for a minute, then replied with a sad tone in her voice, "Kind of like . . . people do to us at church."

Tony looked at his wife in disbelief, but knowing all that their family had been through in churches over the years, he knew what she was saying was true. After a moment, he looked across the yard at his kids who were still playing ball with the remaining birthday guests and said, "Yeah, kind of like that."

Tony was a peacemaker. He done his best to keep peace whenever a conflict arose. When his next-door neighbor was causing trouble, instead of fighting and arguing, Tony treated him nicely even though it was hard to be nice to this neighbor. There were many times that Tony wanted to strike back, get angry, and reciprocate, but he didn't. Tony knew from his childhood how important it was to keep peace among neighbors. He didn't want what happened when he was a kid to repeat itself in his front yard and in front of his kids. He was determined to keep that from happening.

"Live peaceably with all men." Tony would quote this verse to himself from Romans when Grady would threaten to shoot his dogs, get drunk, and cuss his kids or just be obnoxious toward Tony and his family. "Lord, I'm glad you said in that verse 'If it be possible'! I'm trying to 'love my neighbor,' but Grady is making this very difficult."

Grady was so much like Tony's dad Victor that it worried him. That's one of the reasons why Tony went beyond the call of duty to keep peace. The aggressive behavior toward Tony and his family was relentless, and it went on for years. Finally, through divine inspiration or desperation, Tony came up with a plan. Hoping to ease tensions between Grady and his family, Tony asked Donnie to make two of her delicious homemade pecan pies. Donnie was reluctant to make them when she learned who they were for.

"Are you going to put poison in them?" Donnie joked as she was pulling them from the oven.

"It's tempting," Tony laughed. "But I am going to add something special to them."

Donnie has a special recipe for pecan pies that she has kept secret for years, and these delicious desserts have not only earned her a few dollars but have also earned her a few ribbons in baking contests as well. They have also been sold on radio and television shows and even impressed a few restaurateurs. When Truitt Cathy, the founder of Chic-fil-A, tasted a slice of her pecan pie, he was so impressed he offered to help her open her own bakery in McDonough. Still today, many family, friends, and past customers order them at Easter, Thanksgiving and Christmas. Occasionally, she'll give them as Christmas presents, which is always a welcoming and heartfelt gift. But the response is always the same, "This is the best pecan pie I've ever eaten."

Donnie laid the hot pies on the stove top, then turned around and asked curiously, "What's your secret ingredient?" But before Tony could respond, she put her hands on her hips and asked assertively, "What are you adding to my pies?!"

Tony snickered as he responded, "The only thing I'm adding is . . . prayer!"

Donnie smiled and then replied, "That better be all you add!"

Since it was Christmas, Tony figured his neighbor would be more receptive to gifts, so he prayed over the pies and then walked over to Grady's house and knocked on the door. To Tony's surprise, the usually rude and obnoxious neighbor was cordial and invited Tony in. In all the years they had been neighbors, Tony had never been in Grady's house. Tony visited for a few minutes, then he wished his neighbor a Merry Christmas and left. A few days later, Grady saw Tony and told him the pies were the best he'd ever eaten. Tony smiled and said cheerfully, "Glad you enjoyed them, Grady."

Tony's plan had worked! Whether it was the pies, prayer, or a combination of both, Grady's demeaner changed toward Tony and his family. There were no more threats to shoot their dog, no more cussing the kids, and instead of keeping the foul balls that went over the fence into his yard, Grady would toss them back. The change in Grady was instantaneous, and both Grady and Tony's family lived peaceably together until Tony and his family moved a couple of years later.

Tony not only kept peace among neighbors, but he also settled issues with church people, his employees, a few married couples, and even some in his immediate family. Settling conflicts was something he became good at, but his inability to fix the disagreement with his daughter and son was nearly his undoing. He lost sleep, gained weight, his business suffered, and he slipped into a deep depression. Donnie suggested that he talk to someone, so he went to counselling, sought spiritual advice, and even seen a psychologist. The worry, anxiety, and feelings of losing the family that had brought him so much love and happiness created thoughts of suicide, something he hadn't felt since he was a teenager. He had been a mess for two long years. But now that he and Sam were on speaking terms, and having Leah closer but still distant, it brought him hope and much-needed healing. But tonight, Tony is facing another challenge, another conflict, one that's not easily identified, a conflict that's buried deep inside him that's more painful and darker than any conflict he's ever dealt with. It is one that involves many painful memories from his childhood and a conflict that also involves . . . Marilyn.

Things have improved between Leah & her dad since he started writing this book in 2019. Here they are singing together at the last family reunion.

Tony and Mr. Cathy outside the proposed bakery location discussing Donnie's pecan pies.

CHAPTER IV

THE GENTLE GIANT

Things were staying lighthearted outside the viewing room while the family was waiting on Bryan to come open the door. Having the family together took Tony away from the dread he had been experiencing just moments earlier.

"Is Tyler playing fall baseball?" Tony asked Sam, referring to his eight-year-old grandson.

"No sir," Sam responded, "he didn't want to play fall ball since he had a long season, so he's going to take a break from baseball and do some fishing and hunting."

"You can't blame him. Playing two seasons of baseball in one year is rough on teenagers, let alone an eight-year-old."

"I agree," Sam chuckled, "although it never bothered me!"

Tony smiling, "You or Caleb; although that one summer when Caleb played nine games in one week, it really took a toll on him."

"I remember that!" Caleb chimed in. "I didn't want to see a baseball field for a week!"

"I would have loved it!" Sam answered sharply. "I'd have been ready to play nine more the next week."

"Not in that Florida sun!" Caleb chided back. "You wouldn't have lasted six games."

"Yeah right!" Sam answered sarcastically. "I didn't have the chance like you did."

Tony smiled as he listened to his two sons trading jabs at each other over who was the better ball player. This is nothing new. Sam rides

Caleb about not taking advantage of the opportunities he had playing Interstate Travel Ball and college, and Caleb aggravates Sam about throwing his baseball career away over girls. The playful insults and jabs seem to come up every time they're together, and it's been going on for years, and based on what the family and guests are witnessing, it looks like it will continue to go on for many more. It comes from the competitiveness between them and their love for the game of baseball. Both Sam and Caleb now play on church leagues and travel soft ball teams, which, in a way, is a continuation of their baseball careers. And since they both are good and play against each other regularly, the saga of who's the better player will continue.

Tony is glad the legacy of baseball has been passed down to his sons and now grandson. Like Tony, both Sam and Caleb have coached at the high school level, which is quite a credit to their baseball knowledge and skill, and now that Sam is coaching his son's baseball team, it gives Tony a sense of pride and accomplishment.

When Sam was younger, Tony would often pull into the driveway and see his oldest son tossing baseballs up in the air and swinging at them. Tony would blow the horn to make sure Sam saw him so he would stop swinging until Tony had parked his vehicle in a safe place.

Occasionally Sam would convince one of his sisters to pitch to him, but this only lasted until one of them got drilled with a tennis ball or Sam became a bat hog and wouldn't let them hit. Tony would hurry out of his vehicle and head straight to the flat worn-out area in the yard known as the pitcher's mound, even though it wasn't a mound. Tony would pitch, and Sam would hit. This would go on for as long as possible, which was usually until suppertime.

"Supper's done!" Donnie would swing open the door and holler across the yard. "You guys hurry up and come on in!"

But Tony and Sam wouldn't budge. They were on a mission.

"One more, Dad," Sam would plead as he'd swing his bat over the flat rubber home plate in front of the chicken wire back stop. "Right down the middle, Dad. No curve balls."

"Here it comes!"

Crack! This scenario repeated itself day after day, week after week. Sam would hit the ball with such force that the high fly balls would leave the large front yard on Price Drive West in Locust Grove and land in the trees over 200 feet away or sail over the powerlines along the road and land in the neighbor's yard across the street, which was more than 250 feet from the dirt batter's box.

"Another homerun!" Sam would shout as he laid the bat down on his shoulder, admiring the distance.

"Not bad for a twelve-year-old!" Tony would shout proudly in case any neighbors were watching or listening. "That's an easy home run in your ballpark."

"Throw me one more, Dad. One more!" Sam couldn't get enough.

After a few more pitches, the front door would swing open, "Mom said to get in here; supper's getting cold," one of the girls would shout from the porch, then walk back in the house.

"We'd better go in before Mom gets mad at both of us!" Tony would put his arm around his son as they walked down the hill toward the house. "After supper, you need to pick up all the balls scattered around the yard and in the neighborhood."

"I will," Sam would reply. "Can we hit some more after supper, Dad? Can we?"

"We'll see," Tony answered. "But we need to work on your pitching too."

"I can't wait till my next game, Dad!"

Tony would look down at his happy son, smile, and say, "I can't either!"

Because Tony was a minister, and his family evangelized for several years, Sam didn't start playing baseball until he was eleven. Tony signed him up in Locust Grove, and when Sam went through the draft, he landed on the Cardinals, a good team that had been playing together since the boys were seven and eight.

Since Sam was a new player and had never played on a team before, and the coach felt like the new player wasn't very good, Sam sat on the bench a lot. This discouraged the young athlete and frustrated Tony.

Tony shared his frustration with one of the assistant coaches, and he suggested that Tony transfer Sam to Rex Park, where the rules called for a continuous batting order, and every child took turns playing the field. To make sure Sam was able to enjoy the game of baseball he had worked so hard at, Tony signed him up at Rex Park the following year. This proved to be a smart move for Sam.

It was March 1996. While Atlanta was preparing to welcome the Summer Olympic athletes, Tony was preparing his young athlete for the upcoming baseball season. A lot had changed in one year for the father of four and his family. He had purchased a radio station in Morrow, Georgia, in May 1995. Sam and his siblings were now going to a Christian school in Forest Park, so playing baseball at Rex Park worked out great since the park was only a few miles from the radio station and the school. Tony was now working longer hours than usual. He would sometimes be at the radio station as early as 6:00 am and would often work till 8:00 pm. He worked hard trying to pull the radio station out of debt and get it back on its feet, but despite the long hours and his newly acquired responsibilities that came with running a business, he made time for his girls' volleyball matches and his boy's baseball games.

Sam had gone through the draft and landed on the Rockies, a newly formed team coached by Bob Shanahan, who was more concerned about his players having fun than his "won/loss" record. Bob was a gentleman and a great coach. His son was the primary catcher and a good pitcher, and he and Sam immediately became good friends. The season started in early April, and after only two games, the coach moved Sam to the number four position in the lineup known as the "cleanup position." He also placed him in the first base position on the infield and started letting his new, stocky right-hander pitch.

One Tuesday afternoon, Tony finished his radio show at 5:00, but he had to oversee something urgent, so he asked his sports director Dave Pena to drive Sam to the park for his 6:00 game. Tony was hurrying to finish what he had to do, and he finally left the station around 5:55. When Tony walked up to the twelve-and-under field, he greeted Dave, who was standing behind the backstop, and thanked him for getting his son to the field on time. Tony noticed Sam was at the plate already and told Dave, "I got here just in time."

On the very next pitch, Sam swung and hit one of his notorious high fly balls toward right field. Tony and Dave watched as the ball kept climbing higher and higher. When the ball finally came down, it landed on the bank on the other side of the fence. After only having a few at-bats with the Rockies, the young right-hander had hit his first homerun! Tony started jumping and hollering as Sam rounded first base.

"The Cardinals' coach could've seen a few of those last year if he would've let Sam play!" Tony said, gloating as his son went into his first ever homerun trot.

"I'm sure that won't be his last one either!" Dave said confidently. "That kid has some power."

When Sam reached home plate, his entire team was waiting for him. They surrounded him, slapping the top of his helmet, and jumping up and down with excitement. The proud father watched as his son was being donned with congratulations from his teammates, the parents, his coaches, and even some players on the other team. *What a great feeling that must be for Sam*, Tony thought as his mind flashed back to a childhood memory of his own.

"That was quite a shot!" Dave said excitedly. "And he went oppo too!"

Tony responded, "That's Sam's first real home run!"

Dave responded quickly, "You need to go get that ball!"

Tony heeded Dave's advice and headed to the area where the ball landed. He measured the distance between the ball and the fence, retrieved it, and then headed to the dugout where his twelve-year-old was standing by the entrance, still gleaming.

"Way to go, son! Your first homerun! WOW!" Tony said proudly as he handed him the ball.

"That went over the 180-sign, Dad!" Sam replied excitedly.

"I know! I just had walked up when you hit it!" Tony confessed. "The ball landed about ten feet on the other side, which puts the distance at 190 feet."

When Tony told Coach Bob that it was Sam's first homerun, he responded, "We'll have to take everyone to Dairy Queen after the game and celebrate!"

"Do I need to pay for the ball?" Tony asked since he was keeping the prized possession.

"No sir, it's yours!" the coach said happily.

Knowing how important Sam's first homerun was to both him and his dad, Tony had a plaque made with the slugger's individual team picture on the left side and the homerun ball encapsulated and mounted on the right. He also had an inscription put over the ball that reads, "Sam StCyr, April 25th, 1996, 1st Homerun." Though the plaque is covered in dust and stored away in a box in Sam's attic, the memory of that moment is still forever imbedded in Tony's "special" memory bank.

After Coach Bob seen how well Sam could hit, field, and throw, and knowing that Tony had been Sam's primary coach all his life, he asked Tony to help him coach the team, and Tony happily accepted. This was a dream come true for Tony. Even though Tony was busy with the radio station, his love for his son and the game of baseball became a priority, so he helped at most practices and didn't miss any of Sam's games that year.

Tony took his coaching position seriously and started taking coaching classes. By the time Sam was fifteen, Tony had earned his Pro Coach Certification in both baseball and softball. Tony was asked to help coach Sam's high school team after their team finished 0–13 their inaugural year. The next year, they went 13–3, winning the state championship. When Caleb was twelve, Tony decided to coach his own team. He told Caleb he could pick the team's name, and Caleb came up with "The Stingers." Tony coached the Stingers for three years out of Warren Holder Park in Locust Grove, just missing the AABC State Championship in 2007 by one game.

When Caleb was fifteen, he came up with the name "Georgia Spartans" for their newly formed travel ball team. A travel ball team is a team that is made up of elite baseball players who travel from town to town and state to state, playing other travel ball teams. Tony coached the Spartans until Caleb went to college in 2011. During the six years that Tony coached the Georgia Spartans, the team acquired a major league USSSA rating, won numbers of tournaments, spent the night in many cities and states, and the busy father/coach had a lot of fun and experienced many memorable moments with his son, his teammates, and their parents. Tony retired from coaching in 2012.

As Sam grew older, he got taller, stronger, and better. Sam would hit a baseball so hard that Tony started worrying about his long homeruns and line drives breaking car windows or damaging houses. Tony was also worried about being hit as well, so he switched to throwing him tennis balls when they were practicing in the yard. When Sam pitched, his dad would wear catchers gear because Sam's fast ball, sliders, and curves would occasionally miss the mitt and hit Tony in areas that base-balls weren't meant to hit! His side arm curve became so nasty that it was very hard to catch. When Sam was fourteen, he hit a tennis ball so hard that it hit his dad in the shoulder and knocked him to the ground.

"I'm glad that was a tennis ball!" Tony said as he picked himself up off the ground. After Sam saw his dad was ok, he started laughing, and they both still laugh about it to this day. By trying to hit the tennis balls as far as he hit baseballs, Sam's arm strength and bat speed increased a lot. He had become a powerful hitter and a dominating pitcher over time.

When Sam was fourteen and in the eighth grade, he played on the Knights, his high school team, and the Rex Mets, a fourteen-and-under team both at the same time. That was a lot of games for Tony to attend, but he didn't miss a one. He enjoyed watching his son play and helped both his teams as much as he could. He even learned how to keep the score book so he could sit in the dugout or close to home plate.

Sometimes Sam would have a school game and a rec game the same day. His dad loved watching his son navigate from the ninety feet base path at high school to the seventy-five feet base path on the four-teen-and-under rec field. Sam was a fast runner for his size, so stealing second on the ninety feet base path while on the high school field was fairly easy for the lanky long-legged teenager. But when Sam was on the fourteen-and-under rec field, stealing second on the seventy-five feet base path was a cake walk. Tony would smile as Sam stole second on the rec field because it seemed as if his son took only five steps and was standing on second.

Sam won his high school's MVP award five years in a row. He struck out over ninety batters his junior and senior year. His tall frame combined with the side arm delivery that his dad taught him at a young age gave him an amazing advantage over most hitters. He still holds the home run and strike out record at his high school to this day. To honor Sam and his accomplishments, the school retired his number twenty-four after he graduated.

Tony believed Sam had the ability and talent to play at a higher level than high school, so he signed Sam up to play on a travel ball team when he was sixteen. The tall right-hander caught the eye of college coaches when he pitched a game at West Georgia University, where he struck out nine and only gave up two runs.

When he attended a training camp at the University of Georgia, the coaches there were impressed with his size and talent, but since Sam was only in tenth grade, there were rules that kept coaches from talking about recruitment to sophomores. Tony had a couple of professional scouts call about Sam during his senior year.

After graduation, Sam attended an Atlanta Braves tryout and pitched against some great hitters who were also trying out for the Braves. Sam made them look bad at the plate and didn't give up a single hit. The head scout was so impressed with Sam's performance that he told Tony he had put a check beside Sam's name. After the tryouts had ended, the scout asked Sam where he was playing ball, and Sam responded, "Nowhere." The scout looked at Sam and said sharply, "You need to be playing baseball, son," then turned and walked away. That is how Sam's amazing baseball legacy ended.

Once Sam got interested in girls, his baseball aspirations waned. *Puberty has ended many young athletes' career,* Tony thought as he and his son sat quiet on the long ride home from Decatur back to Locust Grove. Tony feels like it must have been what the Lord wanted, although he was hoping Sam would've at least played college ball or made it to the minor leagues.

Sam's first homerun ball.

CHAPTER V

TURTLE

Tony noticed his youngest son wasn't chiming in anymore, so he looked around, then asked, "Where's Caleb?"

Leah chuckled, "In the bathroom. Where else?"

Tony looked down the hall and saw Caleb walking out of the men's room. As he walked toward the group, Caleb noticed the family staring at him.

Caleb knew exactly what they were thinking, so he smiled and said, "Hey! That was a long ride over from McDonough."

Leah responded, "You usually take longer."

Caleb smiled, "Not this time. Just number one!"

Everyone had a good laugh at Caleb's expense, then Caleb walked up to his mom and gave her a soft and gentle embrace. Donnie squeezed Caleb tightly as she told him, "I missed you so much!"

Caleb is Tony and Donnie's baby boy. He was born in 1993, nearly ten years after Sam. Tony told everyone when Caleb was born that he was their "Whoops there he is," a funny twist on a popular song that was released a few months prior to Caleb's birth.

Caleb is taller than his dad but not as tall as Sam; he stopped growing when he hit six-foot-three. He works out at a local gym three days a week and is not only tall but also broad and buff. However, don't let the brawn fool you; he's also smart, intelligent, and the only one of Tony and Donnie's children to attend college. Caleb is talented, built, athletic and good-looking but is still single at twenty-six, something his mom and dad have encouraged him to fix.

When people see younger pictures of Tony, they often say how much Caleb favors him. When people ask Tony where they got their height, he would respond jokingly, "From the Miracle Grow under the sink." Tony would also hold his stomach and say, "I'd be taller too if so much of me hadn't grown outward!" Tony loves the fact both his boys are taller than him. Even today, when he introduces them, he'll say, "This is my little boy Sam" or "This is my little boy Caleb."

Unlike Sam, Caleb started playing baseball at the age of five. He also played at Rex Park. Caleb played T-ball for two years and then played 7/8 for another two years. Tony helped coach Caleb's T-ball team his first year, so when the head coach decided not to coach anymore after that season, Tony decided to coach the team the second year.

One of Tony's fondest memories of Caleb playing T-ball came when they were playing a rival team whose coach passed over Caleb the previous season. Caleb was standing in the short-stop position with one of the opposing teams' hardest hitters at the plate. The coach pitched the ball, and the player hit a screaming line drive right at Caleb, who somehow threw up his glove and snagged the ball out of the air. Tony ran out on the field, picked his young player up, swung him around, and toted him to the dugout. That magnificent play ended the inning and sealed the win for the T-ball Braves.

The next season, Tony carried the young team into 7/8. By that time, Caleb was six and things were going great at the radio station, so his dad had more free time to be the head coach. After two boring seasons of 7/8, Caleb lost interest in baseball and didn't play again until he was eleven.

Since Locust Grove Recreational Department had started the continual batting order like Rex, Tony signed his young son up to play in Locust Grove. Even though Caleb hadn't played in a couple of years, Tony still worked with his young athlete in the yard, although Caleb's interest in baseball was far below the level of his older brother.

When Caleb went through the draft, he landed on the Astros, a local team that was moving up from 9/10, which needed a few players. By now, Caleb had the ability to hit, catch, field, and throw very well, so he was picked in the first round of the draft, but there was one thing the eleven-year-old didn't have that many other players his age had, and that was . . . speed. During one of the team's practices, the coach was working on base running, and he was telling all his players as they ran to, "Get on your horse," an expression used to encourage a player to run faster.

When it was Caleb's turn to run, the coach hollered, "Get on your horse, Caleb!" When Tony saw how hard it was for his young and chunky son to put one foot in front of the other, he hollered, "Get on your turtle Caleb!" This immediately brought laughter from the parents, the coaches, his teammates, and even Caleb. From that day forward, Caleb was crowned with the nickname "Turtle," and Tony still gives him turtle memorabilia today. Tony often joked about his slow son being the only player on the team that could stretch a triple into a single, though it may be hard to believe Caleb was really that slow.

While playing with the Astros, Caleb's attitude about baseball changed, and like his father and brother, he had fallen in love with the game. Where Caleb lacked in speed, he made up for it with his pitching, his fielding, and especially his bat. When the season ended, the Astros coach let everyone know he wouldn't be coaching anymore, so for the next season, Tony took Caleb, Graham Parker, a friend of Caleb's from school, and ten players from the draft, and the Locust Grove Stingers were born. After losing their first three games, the Stingers started playing well together.

Caleb and Graham had become known around the league as the "Dynamic Duo" because of their size and domination on the field. Whether they were pitching or hitting, they were a force to be reckoned with. Tony had Caleb batting third and Graham batting fourth. It was almost automatic; Caleb would get on base, and Graham would drive him in. When the two hitters at the top of the lineup got on base, Caleb would almost always drive them in. When Graham got on base, the hitters behind him would usually drive him in, and so the cycle continued the entire season.

Both Caleb and Graham were much taller than most of the players they pitched against, so when they were on the pitcher's mound, they were quite intimidating. Graham was so big and tall that Tony had to carry his birth certificate with him since he looked older than he was. He never had to show it to any of the other coaches, but he did hear a lot of the other parents and players making comments about how big he was. Tony would ask them if they wanted to see his driver's license, which typically generated a laugh, although some of the coaches on the other teams didn't think it was funny.

The Stingers scored so many runs that year that it was amazing to watch. After the slow start, the Stingers only lost one game the entire season. When the season had ended, Caleb was sporting a .883 batting average while Graham edged him out with a .887 average, quite an amazing accomplishment for any baseball players at any age.

After the All-Star Game which Caleb and Graham both made, Tony entered his Stingers in a World Series tournament in Rossville, Georgia. The second game in that tournament is one of Tony's most memorable games of that year. After the Stingers had taken a beating the night before, many of his players had their heads hanging down as they entered the dugout the following morning for the 9 am game. Tony gave his team a good pep talk, and then they hit the field. The team they were playing that morning was the host team from Rossville, and it was a "win or go home" situation since both teams had lost their first game.

Though tired from playing past 11:00 the night before, the Stingers took the field with a newfound energy. When the game was over, Caleb had gone four for four and led his team to its only victory in the World Series tournament. Tony had a souvenir magazine cover photograph made for his young star to commemorate his accomplishments in that game, and he still cherishes it to this day.

Although Caleb had hit the fence many times during his twelve-and-under season, the all-elusive first home run he was chasing never happened. But it would happen and happen soon, and when it did, it would be a game that Caleb nor his dad would forget!

Caleb and Graham in their Stinger's uniform.

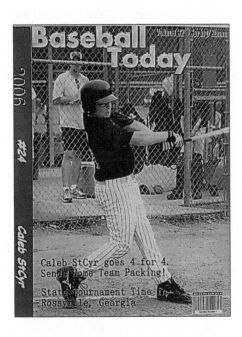

The magazine cover from the World Series in Rossville, GA.

CHAPTER VI

HITS, HOOPS, & HAPPY DAD

T he following year when baseball season rolled around, Caleb was more anxious to play than he had ever been. Since most of Tony's team was young enough to play twelve and under one more year, Tony only had Caleb and Graham when the fourteen-and-under draft started. Tony was able to pick up some great talent from the draft, including a fast runner named Josh. Josh was one of the fastest kids Tony had ever seen. He was tall and had gazelle-like speed. He covered the outfield like a pro and beat out most slow ground balls for singles. He not only stole second and third base with ease, but he also stole home a few times. Saying he was fast was an understatement, but since he had lightning speed, he was an excellent fit for Tony's coaching MO, which is, "get them on, get them over, get them in." Josh's speed earned him a place in centerfield and landed him in the leadoff spot.

Caleb had been growing taller, stronger, and slimmer since he had turned thirteen and was running fast enough to swipe a few bases even though they were now ninety feet apart, fifteen feet farther than they were on the twelve-and-under field. Caleb and Graham had continued their one-two punch from the third and fourth place position in the lineup just as they had done the previous season. Their pitching had improved as well and throwing from the 60.6 feet distance seemed to enhance their control.

Like last year, it took a lot of coaching and a few games to get the newly formed team on the same page, but after the fourth game, they were starting to play good defense and score a lot of runs.

Tony has a lot of great memories of his years coaching at Warren Holder Park in Locust Grove. He still goes back occasionally when no one is there, stares out over the 12U and 14U fields, and lets the memories play out like an uncontrolled video player. But his two favorite memories from his years of coaching, they are ones he will cherish forever.

Caleb was in eighth grade at the time, and being the athlete he was, he had gotten good at golf and had earned a spot on the school's golf team. On the first day of baseball season, Caleb was scheduled to pitch that night against the Elite Braves from McDonough, a travel ball team that was known for beating their opponents and beating them badly. He also had a golf match after school, so Tony wasn't sure how long his young right-hander would be able to pitch since he had walked and played nine holes of golf just a few hours earlier.

As Caleb was throwing his warm-up pitches, Tony told him, "I know you're tired, but just go out there and do your best, and I'll take you out after the third inning." This was the first time the young thirteen-year-old pitched from the 60.6-foot-high school mound. Caleb took the mound, and after three innings, he hadn't given up a hit. His dad asked, "How are you feeling?" and Caleb replied, "I feel great!" Since Caleb pitched the fourth inning without giving up a hit, his dad let him pitch the fifth, sixth, and the seventh.

When the game was over, Caleb had pitched his first no-hitter and had struck out thirteen of the Elite travel ball Braves. Tony was so excited for his young son. "Wow, Caleb! your first no-hitter!" Tony said as he put his arm around him. "If it wasn't for the two walks, you would've had a perfect game," Tony said, expressing amazement in his young son's pitching performance. "Maybe you need to walk and play nine holes of golf before every game you pitch," Tony said jokingly. Caleb smiled and replied, "I may just start doing that!"

Tony's other favorite memory happened not long after Caleb's no-hitter. It was a warm spring night at Warren Holder Park, the Stingers' home field in Locust Grove. The smell of spring was in the air, the park was noisy under the lights as games were being played on all four fields, and children were at the concession stand with their parents ordering drinks and candy.

The field where the fourteen-and-under teams played was the same field the adult leagues played on, so the fences were much farther away from home plate than the other fourteen-and-under fields around the county. As Caleb stepped in the white-chalked batter's box, his dad shouted to his young son from the third base coaches' box, "Hit it hard somewhere, son." As fate would have it, Caleb swung hard and hit a high fly ball to center field. The centerfielder went back, back, back until he ran out of room. "That's . . . GONE! WHOOHOO! FINALLY!" Tony shouted. Caleb had hit his first homerun! Dad was excited, Mom was excited, the parents were excited, and his teammates were excited as they emptied the dugout and stood at home plate as Turtle rounded the bases in a trot he would soon become accustomed to.

As he rounded third, his dad gave him a high five and said, "Great shot, son! I knew you had it in ya!" As he touched home plate, his teammates slapped him on the helmet and patted him on the back as they jumped up and down in celebration.

It was Deja vu for Tony all over again. His mind raced back to when Sam hit his first home run and how excited it was for both him and Sam. After hundreds of at-bats and thousands of swings both on and off the field, Caleb had hit his first homerun. The excited thirteen-year-old headed back to the dugout with his teammates in tow, grinning ear to ear. When the inning was over, Tony walked in the dugout, hugged his son, and said, "You finally did it, and on the biggest field in the county."

"Yes sir, and it's about time. Wait till Sam here's about this," Caleb said with excitement still in his voice.

"I'm sure he already has. Your mom hasn't stopped texting since you hit it!" Tony laughed.

The ball landed over 300 feet from home plate. Andrew Parker, Graham's dad, retrieved the ball and handed it to Tony as he entered the dugout. The proud dad took out a pen and wrote, "1st Homerun," put the date on it, and tossed it to Caleb. As he watched Caleb looking at the ball and showing it to his teammates, he was sad for a moment as he thought about his short baseball career, wishing he had a ball that said, "1st Homerun," but he quickly snapped out of it and began to command his players to take the field. As exciting as Caleb's first home run was, it was not the highlight of the night. There would be a lot more excitement for the young ball player before this game was over.

When Caleb stepped into the batter's box for the second time, he smashed a ball into the left-center field gap and made it all the way to second, a rare double for a kid whose nickname is Turtle. His teammates were almost as excited for his double as they were for his home run! At his next at-bat, he roped a single into left field. The boy was now three for three and only a triple away from "the cycle," a term used to describe a player who hits a single, double, triple, and a home run in one game. As word spread through the stands that all Caleb needed was a triple for the cycle, anticipation was mounting as the young player moved into the on-deck circle for what would certainly be his last at-bat of the game.

Runners were standing on second and third as Donavon, the second-place hitter was taking his practice swings. Graham's dad was standing outside the fence and motioned Tony over and asked, "Do you think the other team will intentionally walk Caleb if first base is open when he comes to the plate?"

"I sure hope not. That will ruin his chance for the cycle. Hopefully, Donavon can reach, and they'll have nowhere to put him."

Tony walked back to the third-base coaches' box, and he and Andrew watched with great anticipation, knowing if first base was open when Caleb came to the plate, the possibility of the opposing team giving him a free pass was real. Everything was hinging on what Donavon, the small but feisty shortstop, would do at the plate.

"Ball four," the umpire shouted as the ball missed low and outside. The second-place hitter dropped his bat and hustled toward first.

"Bases loaded!" Andrew said excitedly. "Now they'll have to pitch to him or walk in a run!"

A hush fell over the anxious crowd as Caleb stepped into the now barely visible right-handed batters' box. He held his right hand up to the umpire to signal time as he dug a little dirt out with his cleat, then stepped out, took a couple of practice swings with his orange and black DeMarini, then checked his dad for the sign. Tony knew a triple would be hard to come by for the slow-running thirteen-year-old pitcher/catcher, but he was hopefully optimistic.

With bases loaded and three hits in the book, including his first home run, a ground out or a sacrifice fly would be okay in Tony's opinion because either will score a run. "Caleb has already put on a show for the home fans and visiting team, so it doesn't matter what he does this at-bat, he's still the star of the night," Tony reasoned as his son was focusing on him for the sign. Tony went through his usual sign sequence, then touched the tip of his cap, clapped his hands, and said, "Just do what you been doing all night, Caleb. Hit it hard somewhere."

Caleb stepped back into the batter's box as the silence became deafening. The pitcher looked in for his sign, went into the stretch, and then pitched. Caleb swung away like his dad had told him. When the ball left the bat, there was no doubt Caleb had missed his chance to hit for the cycle. Everyone knew the young player would have to try for the hard-to-come-by cycle some other time because the ball was hit so hard that it was what baseball players and sports commentators refer to as a "no doubter!"

The ball flew higher and farther than his previous home run and landed in the trees behind the score board in left field. Caleb's mom, the players, and their parents went crazy jumping up and down and hollering! Some parents from the other team and even the coaches and players stood and applauded as Caleb rounded the bases. Tony was emotional as he seen his son being celebrated by the other team, their coaches, and their fans. Tears of joy were forming in his eyes as he tried to maintain his composure while watching his young son trot around the bases for the second time as if he were a pro at it. He gave his son another high five as he stepped on third, but this time, he was speechless, unable to form any words as his excitement, pride, and emotions overwhelmed him.

As Caleb crossed home plate, his teammates surrounded him with more enthusiasm and excitement than they had when he hit his first home run. Tony watched as his son went toward the dugout surrounded by his teammates for the second time in one night, something not many young players get to experience.

In one game, Caleb had hit his first homerun and his first Grand Slam! Since the baseball landed in the woods and ivy approximately 350 feet from home plate, and since there were no lights in the woods, no one was able to retrieve the Grand Slam ball, so Tony wrote on a baseball from the same game, "1st Grand Slam," put the date on it, and handed it to Caleb.

These are some of the memories that Tony loves reliving during his revisits to Warren Holder Park. They are precious to him, and reliving them gives him a sense of purpose and accomplishment as a father and coach. Whenever he is feeling down or depressed, he'll visit Sam and Caleb's high school field or Warren Holder Park and reminisce of the good times he had watching and coaching both his sons as they played the game he eagerly desired to play growing up.

Caleb continued to hit home runs, singles, doubles, and an occasional triple as he pursued the game he had once tried to quit. He played on his high school team, the Georgia Spartans, his dad's travel ball team, as well as other travel ball teams, including the Blaze, Georgia Predators, Foundation Sports, and a missionary baseball team that used baseball to spread the gospel.

Caleb played tournaments in Georgia, Tennessee, Florida, and other states. He played in the Perfect Game in East Cobb, helped his high school team win the state championship his junior year, and he also played in a national tournament on the St. Louis Cardinals and Florida Marlins practice fields in Florida, where he pitched a masterpiece against a highly flaunted corporate sponsored team.

By the time Caleb had graduated high school, he had played in hundreds of games, dozens of tournaments, thrown several no-hitters, and hit numerous home runs, including back-to-back home runs at Warren Holder Park, the same field he hit his first two home runs on.

During his senior year, Caleb received a four-year scholarship to play baseball at Toccoa Falls in Toccoa, Georgia, but just like his brother, he let girls mess with his head, and his performance and desire for the game waned. Caleb left Toccoa Falls after his first year because the coach wanted him to pitch, but Caleb wanted to play first since pitchers didn't get to hit, and Caleb loved to hit. Since they couldn't get on the same page, the coach dismissed Caleb from the team, and this angered Caleb, so he quit the college and baseball, but he did have a great run from age eleven to eighteen, and he did get close to his brother's home run record in high school but fell two home runs short.

Tony's proud of his baby boy having made it to college and for achieving all he achieved. He is also grateful to the Lord for blessing him and his wife with a son late in life.

So, when Sam picks on Caleb for not taking advantage of all the opportunities presented to him, and when Caleb points out that Sam let girls ruin his chance to play at a higher level, they're both right. But nothing will fix the rivalry between the two brothers except maybe a slow pitch softball game. But history has proven that it doesn't matter if they are on the same team or playing against each other, neither will settle the feud; it will only enhance it.

Even though Sam had hung up his cleats after things didn't work out with the Braves, he stayed involved in baseball. He helped his dad coach for a couple of years and even finished going through the coaching certification to become a pro level baseball coach like his dad.

Having one son sitting beside him in the dugout helping him coach and watching his other son on the field implementing the skills that he had taught him since he was old enough to hold a bat was a wonderful and melancholy experience for Tony. Just having the three of them together around a baseball diamond helped ease the deep embedded pain Tony would sometimes feel when he remembered being denied the opportunity to play as a child. But being around the diamond with both his sons ended when Sam found out he could make good money being an umpire. When he learned how much he could make each game, he gave up coaching and started using his baseball knowledge behind the plate and between the foul lines.

The fact that both Sam and Caleb were tall and athletic enhanced their ability to excel in other sports. Both Sam and Caleb played basketball for their school, but other than shooting hoops in the yard, neither had played much. Caleb worked hard learning drills and played a lot during games, but he never developed the moves or skills to be a star player. Sam didn't want to play basketball; he wanted to just focus on baseball. But since he was so tall, the principal, David McCoy, told him if he wanted to graduate, he had to play basketball for the school. Since Sam was only a sophomore and wasn't certain if the principal was serious or not, Sam played basketball. Because his coach, Tim Coleman, had played basketball in college and was so good at coaching, Sam picked up the game fast. He won MVP three out of four years and, over time, learned to like it.

Tony has two favorite memories of Sam's basketball career. One came when they were playing in La Grange, Georgia. Since Sam was scoring a lot of points, the other team kept fouling him. Sam went to the free throw line fifteen times and made fifteen free throws, something pro athletes rarely accomplish.

His other favorite memory came when they were playing a visiting team from Macon. The visiting team dominated the first half. At halftime, Sam's team was down forty-eight to eighteen. The Knights went into the locker room with their heads hanging low. When the team returned, they had a lot more pep in their step and more determination in their purpose.

The visiting team came out of their locker room the way they went in, overconfident and cocky. By the time the third quarter was over, the Knights had outscored their opponents four to one and had pulled within ten points. The visiting team was still not worried; they were laughing and joking and feeling like they had this game in the bag. With one minute left in the fourth quarter, the Knights had pulled within five points, and the visiting team players were beginning to come unraveled!

Then suddenly, it looked as if the Knights' run was over when one of the opposing players who had made several dunks in the game broke free and ran unobstructed and undefended toward their goal. When he got to the basket, he jumped up to dunk the ball, believing he would seal the game . . . but he missed. The ball bounced off the edge of the rim and landed in the hands of the Knights' guard. Lance Abercrombie, who had caught fire the second half, dribbled down the court, stopped at the three-point line shot, and scored!

The Knights were within two with the clock counting down to forty seconds. An opposing player threw the ball in to his teammate, and a Knight player immediately knocked it away. Sam recovered the ball, went for the layup, and scored! The game was tied, seventy-one to seventy-one! The bleachers, benches, and coaches were all up on their feet going crazy, including Sam's parents!

The visiting team led by thirty points at halftime. The opposing coaches, parents, and even the players were trying to figure out what happened! The Knights happened!

An opposing player threw the ball in, and as soon as they did, the Knights fouled him. With only twenty-five seconds left on the clock, the opposing player went to the free throw line with the game on the line. His first shot rolled around and went in. A sigh went across the opposing teams' fans. The young player who is not so cocky now took aim and shot. This time, the ball hit the rim, and the Knights recovered.

With the clock ticking down, the Knight player who recovered the ball threw it down the court to his teammate. After passing it around and avoiding being fouled, the clock ticked down to eight seconds, seven seconds, the coach hollered "SHOOT!" The opposing team was in shock, disoriented, and lost as to what to do. Suddenly, the ball was passed to Sam, and he went up as he had done hundreds of times, laid the ball off the glass, and it fell in the basket.

The opposing player quickly grabbed the ball, stepped out of bounds, and threw it in to his teammate. The teammate who had made several three pointers that game threw the basketball across the court toward their goal. The crowd watched in what seemed to be slow motion. As the ball crossed half-court, the buzzer expired. Win or lose, the Knights had played the game of their life.

Coming back from such a large point deficit was an amazing accomplishment. The players, coaches, and fans stood still as the ball began to descend toward the basket. It was a brick! The ball missed the backboard and the rim. The Knights had won seventy-three to seventy-two!

While the Knights, their fans, and coaches celebrated their win, the opposing players, their fans, and coaches were in shock. Some of the players were stomping their feet in anger as they marched off the court, and some of their fans, mostly parents, were acting out! But both teams eventually lined up and gave "good game" high fives before heading to their locker rooms.

Though Tony was concerned about the atmosphere of the crowd, everyone left the gym without any further incidents. Sam later told his dad that Coach Coleman had thrown a chair and kicked over the water cooler in the locker room during halftime as he and the team had a "come to Jesus" meeting as he called it.

Whether it was fear or motivation, it worked! It was exactly what the Knights needed to lift their spirits and motivate them to play hard, which enabled them to come back from such a large point deficit. Although Sam was good at basketball, he felt he had a better chance of going to college on a baseball scholarship, so his dad helped him sharpen his baseball skills, although Coach Coleman wanted him to focus more on basketball.

Tony wanted to make sure both his boys had a chance to play baseball at a much higher level than he did, so he studied the game, invested time and money in private lessons and baseball camps, and invested in the finest bats, perfect gloves, and nicest cleats. All the hard work and sacrifice paid off. Both Sam and Caleb won their high school MVP awards every year. They both played college level travel ball, and Caleb went to college on a scholarship and played baseball for Toccoa Falls.

More than twenty years after Sam graduated, his record of ninety-one strikeouts in one season as well as his homerun record still stands. Caleb's .413 batting average his junior and senior year is still standing as the best overall average in school history. Tony is proud of both of his sons' accomplishments and feels like it was worth every minute and dime. Being able to see his son's excelling at a game that he loved so much but played so little made Tony very happy.

People often made comments about how Tony was trying to live out his childhood through his boys, but that didn't bother him. He knew the real reasons, and they were tucked away deep inside him with all the memories, disappointments, pain, and anguish, things that pushed him, that caused him to miss work, miss appointments, and even miss a few meals so he could attend his son's games, things that he had been hiding for years, decades, things he would rather not talk about and he'd rather forget but couldn't. He knew the real reasons, and they were more serious and meaningful than anyone could imagine.

After Donnie released Caleb from her bear hug, Caleb walked over and gave his dad a big hug. As Tony and Caleb embraced, Tony jokingly asked, "You had to hug your mama first, huh?"

Caleb smiling, said, "You know it!"

Caleb is definitely a momma's boy. When he was growing up, Tony would often invite him to ride to the store with him, but Caleb would almost always decline. The youngster would run and climb up on the couch that was in front of the big picture window overlooking the front yard, stand up, and say, "I don't want to go. I just want to watch you leave."

Tony thought his young son's behavior was rather odd, but he would honor his wishes, choosing to go to the store alone or with one of his other children rather than to force Caleb to leave his mom. Caleb would wave to his dad as he drove up the driveway and stay in place until his dad was out of sight, then he'd climb down and go back to playing. His words and behavior inspired Tony to preach a sermon entitled, "I Want to Watch You Leave."

Sometimes when Tony had to work out of town for a couple of days, he would invite Caleb to go along, even bribing him with ice cream and pizza, but Caleb would decline, preferring to stay at home with his mom. Tony took Caleb fishing and hunting as he grew up, but he never really took to it like his brother did.

"I don't understand that boy not wanting to go fishing or hunting," Tony would complain to Donnie. "He just doesn't show much interest in either of them."

"You have Sam, and I have Caleb, now you let him alone and go do your hunting and fishing with Sam." This was usually Donnie's response as she ushered her husband and oldest son out of the door.

Caleb did occasionally go hunting and fishing with his dad and brother, and he did catch a lot of fish and shoot a few deer, but he got bored really fast when the fish weren't biting or the deer weren't moving, so Tony reluctantly accepted the fact that it just wasn't his "cup of tea."

Since his young son loved baseball and enjoyed golf, he worked hard to ensure they were able to enjoy those things together even though neither of them puts food on the table. As Caleb grew older, things began to change. Tony would invite his son to play a round of golf and immediately Caleb would ask, "Is Sam going?" If Tony said, "No," Caleb would often decline the invitation, but if Sam were playing, he would eagerly accept. Caleb just seemed to like it better if Sam played with them.

Having a son so young when your older has its drawbacks, Tony pondered. *With me being fifty and him only fifteen, maybe he's embarrassed to be with me being I look more like his grandfather than his father.*

Tony approached Caleb about this, but he denied feeling that way. Tony still kept it in the back of his mind since years earlier, a teenage boy he went to church with who had a father much older than him told Tony he was embarrassed being seen in public with him. But Tony didn't let it keep him from building a solid relationship with his young son.

Since baseball and golf were his passion, Tony worked hard and spent as much time, money, and effort needed to keep him doing those two things he thoroughly enjoyed. Taking Caleb hunting wasn't a total waste of time, as he loves shooting dove and duck hunting. He found game birds to be less boring and much more enjoyable than deer hunting. He goes duck hunting with his brother a lot, but it's been years since he's deer hunted. Tony did talk him into going with him on a three-day deer hunt in Alabama a few years ago, close to where he killed his first deer, but since Caleb didn't see anything, he wouldn't go back.

Caleb has grown into a young man that any parent would be proud of. As a matter of fact, all his children are the type of children that any parent would be proud of. He and Donnie must have done something right. They're all outstanding members of their community, and they're all active in a local church, quite an accomplishment in this age of illicit sexual behavior and promiscuity. Now they are not perfect by any means; they make mistakes and may make more. But the Word of God and the fear of God that Tony instilled in them when they were little helps constrain them from drifting too far from the paths they were taught and the God they love.

The wedding day.

The only known picture of just Tony & his dad together.

CHAPTER VII
ALMOST AN ALL-STAR

At an early age, Tony developed a fascination and a love for baseball. He played pee wee ball when he was six, but he really wasn't that good. He didn't have anyone to play catch or show him how to hold a bat or throw the ball. His dad had zero interest in sports. His only interests were keeping his home up and attending his lodge meetings.

After playing one season of pee wee ball, his dad forbade him from playing any more competitive sports. He told Tony he didn't want him being sold and traded like an animal, and that's what would happen if he made it to the big leagues. Tony didn't understand what he meant by that, so he stayed silent. He knew better than to argue with his dad since he had seen how he treated animals, and he didn't want the same fate to happen to him.

Even though Tony was forbidden to play on organized teams, it didn't keep him from playing baseball with the neighborhood kids. He did get to play on a sanctioned Little League team for a few weeks when he was eleven when his mom and dad separated for the umpteenth time.

Tony and his mom moved in with his Aunt Alice, who was living in Hapeville at the time. Not far from her house was a ballpark, and since it was close enough for Tony to ride his bike to it and it was the start of baseball season and the cost was cheap, Tony's mom signed him up.

Tony's parents separated a lot because they fought a lot. Vic, Tony's dad, hit his mom not long after they were married, but being that Tony's mom was taller than Vic, she hit him back. This surprised Vic. Tony's mom was a country girl raised on a farm in the south in a small shotgun house cooped up with eight older siblings, four of them older brothers, so she knew how to fight.

As far as Tony knows, he never hit her again, but his words were equally abusive and caused a great deal of emotional and psychological damage to both Tony and his mom. Whenever Vic was angry, he would scream and cuss and call her a bitch, whore, slut, and other derogatory names. When he was angry at Tony, he would cuss and call him a "sorry bastard" and a "worthless son of a bitch," not something a small child needed to hear in his tender years of development.

This constant barrage of verbal abuse was harder on Tony than his mom. His mom could scream and cuss back and defend herself, but Tony didn't have the vocabulary or will to fight back like his mom, so he just trembled in silence and fear. When his mom would finally get fed up with the abuse, she would leave, and she and Tony would move in with one of her sisters, either Barbara, Betty, or Alice.

Tony remembers a time when his mom left, and they moved into an upstairs government apartment off Sylvan Road near the Lakewood Shopping Center where his mom worked at Woolworth's, but they didn't live there long before they were back together with his dad. He would always promise to treat her and Tony better, but that only lasted a few weeks, and then the fighting and name-calling would begin again.

Vic never talked about his relationship with his parents or his childhood. Tony met Vic's dad once when he was nine. They visited with him for about twenty minutes, and Tony never saw him again. Vic's mom, Lucianna, lived with Vic's sister, Theresa, so Tony saw her every time they went to visit family in Massachusetts.

Since both of Vic's parents were French Canadian, all the grandkids called them Meme and Pepe. Tony learned later in life that his Pepe drank heavily and would come home drunk and beat Vic, his sisters, and Meme frequently. Pepe was jailed for child abuse, including sexual abuse, but secrets and rumors abound as to who the victims of the sexual abuse are. After putting up with William's drinking and abuse for years, Lucianna divorced him when Vic was sixteen. Could this be the reason Vic was angry? Is this why he was abusive to his own family? Only Vic knows the answers to these questions.

Tony liked it when his dad and mom separated! Tony saw it as a vacation from fighting and abuse. His mom would smile more, talk to him more, and they would do things together. Tony would discover a freedom when they were separated that he didn't experience when his mom and dad were together. He couldn't explain it, but he felt good, happy, and free. So, when his mom would go back to Vic and the abusive environment, Tony didn't understand.

"Why would she leave every few months and then go back?" he would ask himself. "It doesn't make sense." Tony was hoping the name-calling and abuse was finally over, but only time would tell.

Living with his Aunt Alice allowed Tony to play baseball again, and that made him very happy. This time, he was on a sanctioned Little League team, and even though the field was mostly dirt, it was better than not playing at all. Tony's baseball skills had improved since pee wee ball, and even though he hadn't played on an organized team in five years, he was more confident than ever in his abilities as a player. He was still a little scared of being hit by a pitch, but he learned to settle his nerves by talking to the pitcher when he stepped up to the plate. And since he could catch and field pretty good, the coach started him at first base.

Playing yard ball has paid off! Tony thought to himself as he dove to his left, smothering a ground ball heading to right field. Then as if he'd been practicing this play for years, he picked up the ball with his right hand, sat up on his knees, and lunged toward first base, tagging the base with the ball just ahead of the speedy runner!

Hearing the crowd roar and clap surprised Tony.

"Great play, kid!" Tony looked over in the stands shyly and smiled, not knowing who said it. Other praises were coming from the third base line from parents and fans from the other team.

"Way to go kid!" a fan shouted.

"Nice play" came from an opposing parent.

Several other congratulatory comments were being directed toward the now embarrassed but happy eleven-year-old.

I wish Mom could be here to see me play, Tony thought to himself as he walked back to his position, scanning the stands for his mom, knowing she was at work but hoping she was there anyway.

Since all of Tony's games were on Saturday, and his mom worked on Saturday, she didn't get to attend many of his games. To this day, Tony can't remember one game his mom attended that season, but he does remember in detail what happened the previous year when he was ten.

Tony's fifth grade class was performing a special dance presentation at Tara Stadium in Jonesboro, the same stadium that the area schools football games were played in, so this was a huge moment for Tony. His mom dropped him off and told him she had an errand to run, but she would be back before his class performed.

All the classes from Hendrix Drive Elementary, including kindergarten through sixth grade, were performing different period dances in front of the parents, faculty, and their guests. Since fifth grade class was next to the last to perform, Tony assumed she would have plenty of time to run her errand and be back for his performance. All the students were decked out in their appropriate period dress, and all the classes had worked hard on their costumes and dance moves for this highly anticipated school presentation.

Tony's class was decked out in fifties attire. Girls were in different colored poodle skirts with matching tops, white oxford shoes, and lacy socks, while the boys were sporting straight-leg rolled-up jeans with unbuttoned shirts over white t-shirts and greasy slicked back hair.

Tony's dancing partner was Yvonne Wimpy, and they had their jitter bug moves down to a tee. Tony had never danced with a girl before, and when they were practicing their dance moves, he would have to hold her hand and put his arm around her waist. This made him have a funny feeling in his stomach, but he liked Yvonne and was glad she was his partner.

While he was dancing to "Rock around the Clock" with Yvonne, he was imagining how excited his mom must be to see her son dancing the dance from her era.

I hope she's taking lots of pictures, he thought as he watched the flash bulbs going off in the stands. Since the stadium lights were bright, he couldn't see who was in the stands, but he was certain his mom wouldn't miss this performance he had worked so hard on.

After the dance was over, his mom met him at the designated area for fifth grade pick-up. "Did you see me, Mom? Did you see me? Weren't me and Yvonne great? Did you get some pictures?" He was so excited!

She waited till they were away from the other parents, and as they walked to the car, she said, "No son, I missed it."

"What? You said you'd be back!" Tony shouted loudly. His mom could tell he was upset.

"I thought I would, but I went to see if your dad was running around on me, and when I got back the sixth grade class . . ."

Tony didn't hear anything else. He melted with disappointment as he done so many times. Something about her spying on his dad . . . "Maybe next time . . ." "Blah blah blah . . ."

"How could you miss this, Mom?!" Tony said with a tone she had never heard. "This dance was important!" Tony was upset and rightly so.

"You watch your tone with me, young man," she responded. "I told you . . ." More blah blah blah is all Tony heard on the way back to the car.

CRACK! The sound of the bat brought Tony back to reality . . . and the game. A hard-hit grounder to third, a throw across the diamond to Tony, who makes the scoop, and the runner is retired.

"Out three. Switch sides!" the umpire shouted as Tony and his team ran to the dugout.

As he was entering the dugout, his teammates were patting him on the back and bragging about the exceptional play he had made at first base. His coach gave him five, and some of the parents were still chatting about it in the stands. Tony was wishing his mom could've seen him so she'd really know how good he had gotten. But as fate would have it, after only a few weeks, Tony's mom and dad worked out their differences, and he didn't get to finish the season. When he told his coach he had to quit the team and why, his coach was disappointed but assured Tony that he understood. The coach could tell Tony was upset about quitting the team, so he tried to cheer him up.

"I just want you to know, Tony," the coach paused, "you made the All-Star team! I was going to tell you later when I told the other players, but you look like you could use some good news."

Overcome with excitement, Tony looked up at the coach and said, "REALLY?! That's great news! Thanks, Coach!"

"You earned it," the coach responded. "You worked and played really hard. I hope you can at least come back and play in that game!"

The All-Star team! Tony thought, *I'm an ALL-STAR!*

Tony knew that the All-Star team was made up of the best players from each team, and now he was recognized as one of the best players on his team! He was so excited! "All-Star!" Tony said out loud. "It had such a nice ring to it." "All-Star, All-Star, I'm an All-Star. I made the ALL-STAR Team!" Tony kept saying it over and over as he was heading to the parking lot where his mom was waiting in the car to pick him up. When he saw the car and his mom sitting inside, the reality hit him. With his parents getting back together, would he get to come back and be an All-Star?

Maybe they'll let me stay with Aunt Alice until the season's over, he thought. *Surely, they'll understand how important this is to me, playing in my first ALL-STAR game.*

Tony had never been recognized at excelling at anything before. He was always the last kid picked in kickball, football, and other activities. He did finish third at summer camp once in a swimming contest, but that didn't rise to the level of being a baseball "ALL-STAR," and he didn't get a trophy for it!

Trophy! I'll get a trophy if I play in the ALL-STAR game! Tony thought.

As Tony got closer to the car, he kept trying to work out scenarios in his mind, how they could get back together, and he could still play in the All-Star game! When he got to the car, he told his mom that he had made the ALL-STAR team and asked if he could come back and play the one game so he'd get a trophy.

"You know how your father feels about baseball, son. He's not going to let you play."

"Well, it's not fair! You go live with him, and I'll stay with Aunt Alice, at least until the season is over, then I can come home."

"You can't stay with Alice. She has to work. Plus, who would drive you to the field?"

"I'll ride my bike like I'm doing now!" Tony responded. "Can't you see how important this is to me, Mom? You can drive me back for just one game, can't you? It's not that far from our home to here . . . PLEAASSE?!"

"I'll talk to your father about it, and we'll see."

Tony knew what that meant. He had heard those words before, and more often than not, his dad won out. As the car pulled out of the parking lot, Tony looked in the back seat and saw all his belongings. He didn't have to ask; he knew where they were heading. Tony sat silent on the way back to the apartment. He kept thinking about being an All-Star and hoping he'd get to return to the field and play in the All-Star game, and more importantly, get a trophy that he had truly earned. *To have a trophy, especially an All-Star trophy sitting on my bookcase, would be wonderful!* Tony thought as he pressed his face against the passenger window to keep his mom from seeing his tears. Tony doesn't know if his mom and dad ever discussed letting him come back and play in the All-Star game. He just knew he never returned to the field and never received his trophy, which really disappointed the youngster and caused additional hurt and pain to his young life and furthered his frustration with his parent's tumultuous relationship.

When Tony's mom finally left his dad for good, they moved to Cartersville, a small town about forty miles north of Atlanta. She had taken a management position at the Woolworths' lunch counter in town. For her moving to a new store and promotion to manager, she had received a significant raise, which allowed her to qualify for her first home. She decided that she and Tony would live in Kennesaw, a small rural town seventeen miles south of Cartersville. She had picked out a lot on a cul-de-sac in a new subdivision about ten miles off of I-75.

While the house was being built, they lived in a small space inside a boarding house within walking distance of her new job. A few months later, they moved into their brand-new home. Tony's mom had always wanted a new home. Vic had promised to buy her another house while they were living in apartments, but something would always come up at the last minute. But now she was free, independent, and prospering. Buying her own home would show Vic that she didn't need him anymore. She also bought a brand-new Dodge Demon. She was determined to show her ex that she didn't need anything from him, except, of course, his child support payments, which he paid faithfully. The promotion, a new car, and a new house would show him. What more could a new divorcee need for her and her son? Obviously for Tony's mom . . . it wouldn't be enough!

The author at bat in his Angel's uniform when he played Pee Wee baseball.

Tony with his pet bird Pepper. He acquired it during the time his mom and dad were separated. He had to leave it with a relative when his parents got back together.

Christmas Party for employees at FW Woolworths.

The lunch counter where Tony's mom worked at FW Woolworths in Cartersville, GA.

CHAPTER VIII

DAD, PLEASE STOP

Tony was thirteen when they moved into the new house in Kennesaw. He was happy for all the extra room the three-bedroom ranch provided them. His mom had one bedroom, but Tony had the other two, one to sleep in and one he used as his own private den. He was happy for the new car he had to ride in, and he was happy for the new thirteen-inch black and white TV he had in his private den. But most of all, he was glad the abuse was finally over.

His dad had always been verbally abusive to Tony, and he got whacked around and spanked with a belt growing up, which was common discipline in those days. His mom also believed in corporal punishment, but knowing what her husband was capable of when he was angry, it exceeded her definition of "corporal punishment." She had heard how he disciplined Joyce and Ginger when they were younger, often turning the belt around and whipping them with the buckle, which was one of the reasons they lived with their mother most of their lives, so whenever his mom was around and Vic was whipping Tony, she would take the belt out of his hand before he went too far. When Tony was four, he remembers her having to take something else away from him that no child should ever have to be disciplined with!

One evening after supper, Tony was watching the newly acquired, color console television set that had just been delivered that day. He was sitting cross-legged in the floor just a few feet from the large screen, watching his favorite show, completely entranced by the new color images. When the urge to use the bathroom hit him, he didn't want to miss anything, so he messed in his pants. Being he had been potty trained for more than two years, this was obviously unacceptable.

When the show was over, he told his mom what he had done, and she took him to the bathroom to clean him up. After taking his clothes off, she went to his bedroom to retrieve a clean pair of underwear. While she was gone, his dad came into the bathroom, picked up the soiled underwear, and started trying to rub them in Tony's face. Tony covered his face with his hands and began to scream. When his mom heard the commotion, she ran into the bathroom and snatched the underwear out of his dad's hand.

"Give me back that underwear! This is how you break dogs from shitting in the house. You rub their nose in it!" Vic shouted angrily as he tried to take the underwear back from her.

"He is not a dog, and you ARE NOT going to rub his nose in anything! He's a kid, for God's sake!"

"I guarantee he'll never do it again! Now give me that underwear! He's old enough to know better!"

Tony stood listening as his mom and his new dad went back and forth, cussing, arguing, and screaming at each other. He believes this was their first argument as husband and wife, and it was over him. He had never heard or witnessed anything like it before. Being he was still dirty, naked, and afraid, he didn't know what to do.

Finally, after a few minutes, his dad left the bathroom, and his mom finished cleaning him up. She took him to his bedroom, put on his pajamas, and tucked him in bed. Tony doesn't remember a lot that went on when he was four, but he does remember that incident quite vividly, and he is so thankful that his mom was at home, or there might have been a different outcome.

Vic's lack of self-control was finally unleashed on Tony one morning at their townhome on Hendrix Drive in Forest Park. Since it had only been a few months, the events were still fresh on his mind, and every detail began to resurface as he tried to watch his favorite afternoon TV show. He tried to suppress them, but they kept pushing through. Like an old television rerun, it would return and replay over and over in his mind. It sometimes resurfaces today. It's the one event that changed his life, his mom's life, and that led to the divorce, the new home, the new car, and this newfound freedom.

Tony wasn't feeling well one morning, so his mom told him to stay in bed and rest. He didn't want to miss school, but since he was sick, he didn't have a choice. He liked school, he liked learning, he liked his teachers and some of his classmates, but he was particularly fond of a cute blond in a different sixth grade class named Rene Whittington. She was his first childhood crush. She had long, curly blond hair that flowed down her back, and she always wore the prettiest dresses. Since they were in different classes, he rarely got to interact with her. He'd pass her in the hall on the way to lunch, or he would see her on the playground during recess, but they were always on different parts of the playground.

Tony would try to sit beside her in the hall during air raid drills, or he would stand beside her outside during fire drills, but since he was shy, it was hard for him to speak to her. He would mostly smile, and she'd smile back, but the lack of conversation didn't stop him from liking her. When he found out she was a student patrol, Tony signed up to be a patrol. He was thinking he'd be able to talk to her since he had seen other patrols walking to their posts together before and after school. But since they were always patrolling on opposite sides of the school, this didn't work out either, so he gave up.

Tony started first grade when he was five years old. His mom insisted he was too smart for kindergarten and told the school principal that his dad didn't believe in kindergarten, so they wanted him to be placed in first grade. Against his better judgment, the principal agreed to their demands. This proved to be a terrible decision for Tony. Since most of his classmates were six going on seven, Tony was always the youngest, smallest, and least athletic of the boys in his class. This made him vulnerable to the tricks and taunts of the other kids. He couldn't kick a ball as good as the girls! He couldn't compete with the boys on the monkey bars, so he was bullied and picked on a lot. He will tell you to this day that his first four years of school were brutal! They were the worst four years of his life. It was only when he reached the fifth grade that he began to equal the size and stamina of the other kids, but his muscle structure and athletic ability was still behind the older boys. His parents didn't know about this because Tony didn't tell them, and today he still doesn't talk about those early school years.

When Tony's mom called to check on him around 11:00 that morning, he told her he was feeling better and asked if he could go fishing. There was a pond behind their complex that he enjoyed fishing in. It had a lot of different fish that a twelve-year-old could easily catch. She gave her approval since it was too late to go to school but quickly added, "Be sure you're gone before 12:00 in case your dad comes home for lunch."

Tony replied with a firm, "Yes, ma'am."

Tony had gotten dressed, grabbed his fishing rod and tackle box, and was heading down the stairs to grab a quick bite before heading to the pond when suddenly the front door opened, and his dad came in. Most of the time, his dad took his lunch since he never knew what part of town he would be working in, but occasionally he would come home for lunch if he was working nearby and, unfortunately, this happened to be one of those days.

Victor was known to most everyone as Vic. He was a World War II veteran and served as a cook in the US Army. He also served as an SP guarding German prisoners of war, which he did much of his Army career. He spoke fluent French, a lot of German, and some Italian. He wasn't very tall, only five-foot-six, which was three inches shorter than Tony's mom. He was strong for his size and weight and was meticulous when it came to detail and organization. He had a head full of hair that he parted in the middle and combed straight back.

Vic didn't talk much about his time in the service, but it was evident by his behavior that he had some anger control issues. He was fifteen years older than Tony's mom, and he was very controlling of her and Tony. Tony had to eat everything on his plate before leaving the table and couldn't drink anything, not even a swallow until he had finished eating all his food. Vic hated animals. Tony had never had a pet other than fish. Tony didn't realize how bad his dad hated animals until he was six years old, and he learned up close and personal.

On a sunny Saturday afternoon, Vic was changing the oil in his work truck. As an electrician for the City of Atlanta, he was on call twenty-four hours a day, so his boss let him drive his work truck home. Having a second vehicle in the driveway in the early sixties was rare and considered a sign of luxury, so to repay the city for their kindness, Vic would keep the oil changed and handle other light maintenance jobs.

His neighbor across the street also worked for the City of Atlanta driving a garbage truck, but the city wouldn't allow Mr. Race to drive his garbage truck home, so he felt Vic was getting special treatment from the city, and this made him jealous. He would express his unfair treatment to Vic, but it fell on deaf ears. Vic was an austere man from New England, a pure Yankee, and a hardened soldier. Mr. Race's petty feelings didn't rattle Vic, and he frankly didn't care what he thought, so he ignored him at least until Mr. Race drove his stinky garbage truck home and started parking it in his yard.

The odor was creating quite the stink in the neighborhood. No matter where you lived, even on other nearby streets, when the wind shifted, you were doused with the stench. During the week and on weekends, Vic and Mr. Race shouted quite a few unpleasant words back and forth across the street with Vic shouting about the stench, and Mr. Race about it being unfair! But after the city was bombarded with complaints from the neighbors, he was forced to leave his nasty-smelling truck at work, and Polar Rock Place returned to normal. But that didn't last long!

Being a curious six-year-old, Tony crawled underneath the jacked-up truck to see what his dad was doing. Tony had crawled on his belly under the truck near the driver's side rear tire with half his body still outside of the truck. His dad was lying on his right side under the engine behind the front passenger tire. Tony could see his dad had oil on his hands, and he was looking for something in the catch pan or on the ground, so he just watched as he maneuvered around in the tight area.

Vic loved his home. He wouldn't dare let any oil get on his cement driveway if he could help it. If it did, he would clean it up immediately. He took care of everything he owned, especially his 1957 Chevy Bel-Aire, which was still in pristine condition after eight years. Even the living room and kitchen furniture would last for decades without needing reupholstering. His front yard was always cut and manicured, and the tall hedges were trimmed and shaped. He kept his yard and home immaculate inside and out.

As you drove down Polar Rock Place from the north, the house sat sixty feet off the road on the right. It was a red brick ranch with three bedrooms, one bath, a large living room. and a small kitchen with a small metal dining table with four chairs. It was easy to identify as you drove down the street since the driveway was connected by a concrete drain to the Johnson's driveway on the left.

The home on the right was owned by the Odom family. The Johnsons and the Odoms both had children around Tony's age, and they would often play together. The concrete driveway ran to double gates that opened to a fenced back yard that was more than twice the size of the front yard.

When someone would ask Vic why he didn't like animals, he would tell them without hesitation, "I hate stepping in dog shit!"

Whenever guests would come over and compliment Vic on the yard, the conversation would quickly turn to dog excrement. He would start by complaining about his neighbors' dogs and cats running loose, and then he'd say, "We don't even own a dog, and every time me or the wife cut the grass or work in the yard, we're stepping in someone else's dog shit." It was Vic's pet peeve. "I work hard to keep this place looking nice, and my neighbors let their dogs out, and instead of shitting in their own yard, they come into mine and do it!"

Vic constantly complained to the neighbors about their dogs coming into his yard, but his complaints fell on deaf ears, so he started placing chards of broken glass in raw hamburger meat for unleashed dogs to find. If he was home, he'd run them out by chasing them or throwing rocks at them. Whether this was the only reason he hated animals or not, no one will ever know, but his disdain for all animals was something he didn't hide from anyone, including his neighbors!

"Found it!" Vic said as he rolled back over on his back.

"Found what?" Tony asked.

"The oil pan bolt," Vic grunted as he wiped off the oily bolt he had just retrieved from the catch pan.

As Tony was watching his dad with great interest screwing the pan bolt in, a cute fuzzy puppy came running underneath the truck between Tony and his dad, wagging its tail and wanting to play. But instead of coming over to Tony, the puppy went over to Vic and started licking his face. Tony's dad went ballistic.

"Get out of here you son of a bitch!" Vic shouted, but the puppy just kept on licking him.

"I said, 'GET OUT OF HERE!'"

Vic rolled back over on his side and picked up a brick with his left hand and started beating the puppy in the head! Tony could not believe what he was seeing. As he was hitting the little dog with the brick, the puppy laid down and looked at him as if to say, "Why are you doing this to me?" The puppy kept licking Vic's right hand that was stretched out away from him while Vic continued to strike the dog with the brick. Tony was certain his dad would stop. *Doesn't Dad know the puppy just wants to play?* But he didn't stop. Tony laid there in shock as his dad beat the innocent puppy until it laid lifeless and still. When Vic saw the puppy was finally dead, he looked up and saw the horrid look on his son's face but showed no remorse.

Tony scooted out from under the truck and ran into the house screaming and crying for his mom. But Mom wasn't home! Tony didn't know where his mom was; all he knew was he was home alone with a dog killer. He went to the living room picture window and watched his dad carry the fuzzy bloody puppy to the end of the driveway and drop it in the street as if he was sending a message to the neighbors who let their dogs roam the neighborhood. Vic then walked back to his truck and finished changing the oil as if nothing had happened. Tony ran into his bedroom and shut the door. *How could Dad do such a thing?* Tony thought as he sat on the hardwood floor with his arms wrapped around his legs and his chin on his knees, leaning against the side of his bed. "Please hurry home, Mom," Tony whispered as he reached and grabbed his favorite stuffed animal. He pulled the black and white fuzzy dog close to him and squeezed it tightly as if he were protecting it from his dad.

News traveled fast on Polar Rock Place. It wasn't long before the neighbors heard what had happened, including the neighbors who owned the puppy. Tony could hear a loud commotion in the front yard as he was hiding from his dad in his bedroom. He wiped the tears from his face and emerged from his room, slowly walking back to the picture window. He saw some people standing in the street crying and holding the lifeless puppy. He could also hear them cussing his dad as well as his dad cussing at the neighbors and blaming them for allowing their dog to roam the neighborhood. The police eventually were called and a report was filed, but nothing was done. According to the police, Tony's dad was in the right. According to Tony, his mom, and the rest of the neighborhood, Vic was a sick and evil man. And that was only the beginning!

The next week, Tony was playing in the front yard with one of the Odom boys when Freddie Race, Mr. Race's youngest son, and two other boys all around the age of twelve were standing in the street, throwing rocks at Tony. Since Tony was only six, he thought they were playing a game, so he picked up the rocks and threw them back to them. The rocks that Tony was throwing weren't going very far, but the rocks the boys were throwing were landing close to Tony.

While Tony was about to throw a rock back, a rock hit him in the forehead and split his head wide open. Tony fell backward to the ground and grabbed his forehead as the boys scattered to their homes. When Tony saw blood on his hand, he jumped up and ran into the house, screaming and crying, something he was starting to do a lot lately. His mom prepared a wet towel with ice and rushed Tony to the emergency room. Tony had to have five stitches. When his mom learned that two of the boys were children of the dog owner and the other boy was Freddie Race, she called the police. The families were ordered to stay away from each other, and Tony's mom told him to play in the backyard from now on since it was fenced and surrounded by bushes. Tony was confused. He hadn't hurt the puppy, why did they hurt him? And why was he being restricted to the backyard? He hadn't done anything wrong.

A few days later, Vic went to crank his 1957 Chevy Belair that he kept in pristine condition, but it wouldn't turn over. He phoned a wrecker and had it taken to his local mechanic shop.

"I bet someone put sugar in the gas tank!" Vic said to the family as the wrecker pulled out of the driveway.

"If they did, the engine's destroyed," Tony's mom responded angrily.

The mechanic confirmed their suspicions. Someone did put sugar in the gas tank, destroying the engine completely. The law was called and a report was made, but nothing could be done since none of the neighbors would confess to seeing anything. Fortunately for the family, Vic believed in full coverage insurance, so he was able to make a substantial down payment on a brand-new Pontiac Tempest from the insurance money he received, which was certainly not the outcome the perpetrators were expecting.

The shiny green sedan was immediately affixed with a locking gas cap and parked closer to the house. Although that was some consolation for the family, it did not ease the hostility they had for the perpetrator. A short time later, some mail came up missing from their mailbox. It was discovered that Freddie Race was the culprit, so the police were called to the neighborhood again. Since stealing mail was a federal offense, the youngster was in big trouble, but when the federal agents learned that Freddie was coerced by an adult, the heat was taken off him and placed on the true conspirator.

Other aggressive behavior was directed toward the family. Someone drove their car through the yard, spinning the tires to mar the pristine yard, and the new car and the house were egged. It just seemed that the neighbors were not going to let the killing of the puppy be forgotten . . . or forgiven. This once quiet and friendly neighborhood had become hostile, and the violence would continue until someone moved or was carried away in a police car or ambulance!

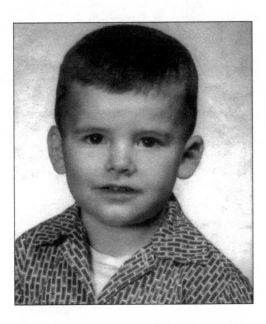

Tony at 3 years of age around the time his mother married Vic.

The house on Polar Rock Place in south Atlanta.

Five-year-old Tony with the older boys and girls in first grade class. He is seated second from the end on the front row.

Both Hendrix Drive 5th Grade Classes at the Capital with Governor Lester Maddox.
Can you pick out Renee? (Hint- Behind the man with the name tag). He didn't
have a chance.

The new 1965 Pontiac Tempest bought after the sugar was put in the gas tank of the
1957 Chevy Belair.

CHAPTER IX

THE NEIGHBORHOOD CRUMBLE

Vic's daughters, Ginger and Joyce, lived mostly with their mother in Massachusetts. Since Ginger, the youngest of the two, liked the milder winter weather in Georgia and the local high school near Lakewood, she would come live with her dad in September and then return home after the school year ended in the spring. It had been a few months since the puppy incident, and things in the neighborhood had settled down. No one had made peace, but at least no one was at war . . . at least not yet.

It was a perfect fall evening on Polar Rock Place in late September. The stars were shining, crickets were chirping, and the smell of fresh-cut grass was permeating through the air as the dew that had just fallen on the freshly manicured lawn was reflecting tiny specs of light like miniature stars from the bright porch light that was mounted on the left side of the front door.

Vic and Ginger had just stepped outside and sat down on the cement stoop to drink some iced tea and enjoy the beautiful evening. Tony had just walked outside and was standing behind them when a cat jumped out of the hedges and into his dad's lap. Instantly and without hesitation, Vic grabbed the cat by the tail, stood up, and began to swing it over his shoulders and from side to side, beating the poor cat's head on the concrete step below him. Tony counted one, two, three, four, five times that he hit the cat's head against the concrete step. Then he slung it hard as he could toward the Race's front yard, and it landed in the paved road under the streetlight. Tony watched in horror as the cat flipped and flopped and turned over and over until it finally laid still and quiet.

"They need to keep their damn pets in their own yard!" Vic blurted out as he sat back down and started drinking tea as if nothing had happened. Tony ran into the house, crying and screaming for his mom and telling her through the tears what his dad had just done. His mom was in utter shock. She came outside and began to scold Vic for what he had done, telling him that we were going to have to move now, didn't he learn his lesson, and other words that Tony rarely heard come from his mother's mouth. This type of trauma was quite a lot for an adult to handle, much less an eight-year-old kid. He ran into his room, scared, frightened, and confused. He had never seen anything suffer like that before. And not only has he witnessed the death of two animals, but he also seen them killed with his dad's bare hands. Tony was truly traumatized by these events, but the fallout from the death of the puppy would be trivial compared to what is about to happen next!

The very next night following supper, a crowd of angry neighbors started gathering in the street in front of the red brick ranch where the fuzzy puppy and the black cat had met their untimely death. Tony had just sat down in the living room floor and started building things with his Lincoln Logs when he heard a commotion outside. His mom, dad, and sister were still in the kitchen cleaning up supper dishes and were not able to hear the ruckus coming from outside, so Tony got up and went to the big picture window. When he moved the heavy drape to the side, he noticed a large crowd of people standing in the street, some carrying sticks, others holding bricks and many of them shouting obscenities toward the StCyr home.

"You can pick on a poor innocent animal, then come out here and pick on me, you worthless piece of shit!"

Other similar comments were being shouted as the anger in the crowd began intensifying.

Tony hollered, "Come 'ere Dad, the neighbors are outside in the street with sticks and rocks!"

Vic peeked out the window, then jerked open the front door and stepped out on the concrete stoop and began shouting and cussing back at the large crowd that were inching ever so closer to the edge of his yard. Among them were Mr. Race, his three sons, including Freddie, their two daughters, the owners of the puppy, and other people from the neighborhood Tony did not recognize. The shouting back and forth intensified with an occasional brick being thrown, landing near the house. When Ginger heard the threats being made against the family, she walked out on the porch and stood by her dad as a sign of solidarity. The angry mob stepped into the yard, hitting their sticks in their hand, and waving their bricks at the unarmed family.

"Get off my lawn!" The five-foot-six stocky, muscular man shouted as he started down the steps toward the agitators.

"Come make me!" The same shout was returned by several in the crowd.

Tony walked out onto the cement stoop and stood by his sister while his mom was calling the police. There were no emergency numbers like 911 or touchtone phones in the 1960s, so dialing the police station on a rotary phone, giving the dispatcher the address and directions to the house, and the reason for the call took a lot longer than it does today, so she was on the phone for some time.

As the crowd crept closer to the house, their anger and the derogatory insults at the entire family intensified. Since Vic was a World War II veteran who fought Germans tougher than them and wasn't afraid of this stick and brick-wielding crowd, he charged straight toward them with nothing in his possession but his balled-up fists, years of frustration, and rage. The crowd immediately jumped Vic as he approached and began wielding their sticks at the brave veteran. He swung and fought with all his might and was able to get a few solid hits on Mr. Race and a few of the others before they finally knocked him to the ground.

Mr. Odom, the next-door neighbor, seeing that Vic was on the ground being kicked and hit repeatedly, ran into the fray to the defense of his neighbor, not that he was defending his behavior, but knowing he was unarmed and outnumbered, was either trying to stop the fight or help even the odds. The angry crowd quickly turned on the defenseless brave man, and he was soon overpowered and thrown to the ground and was being hit and kicked alongside Vic.

When Ginger seen what was happening to her dad and Mr. Odom, she immediately ran down the steps to their defense, demanding they let them go. One of the daughters of Mr. Race threw a brick as she stepped into the grass, splitting the teenager's head open and knocking her to the ground. Both sisters immediately jumped on the bleeding sixteen-year-old and began calling her vulgar names as they punched her with their fists. Ginger curled up in a fetal position, covering her head and face with her hands and forearms, trying to defend herself as the sisters took turns hitting her. After seeing they were unable to punch or slap her in the face, they began pulling her hair out by the handfuls.

Freddie Race who was nearly a teenager now, was standing in the yard screaming at the eight-year-old to come down the steps and fight him like a man. As Tony was watching the horror unfold before him from the cement porch, he was in shock and unsure of what to do. "Should I go down the steps and help my dad and sister? I've never been in a fight before." As Tony was trying to decide what to do, he felt a hand grab his arm and pull him back inside the house. His mom told him not to go back on the porch, and she shut the door and locked it. Tony noticed his mom was holding a large kitchen knife, which startled him.

"The police are on their way!" she said nervously as they watched the commotion through the large picture window.

"I'm scared, Mom." Tony said with a quiver in his voice. "Are they going to kill Dad, Mr. Odom, and Ginger?"

"God, I hope not!" his mother answered, "but if the police don't get here soon, they may!"

It seemed like an eternity before the police arrived, but it was only a few minutes from the time the call was made until the black and white patrol cars from the city of Atlanta arrived. Several cars entered Polar Rock place from the north end of the street with a couple pulling in from the south end with sirens blaring and the red bubble light on the roof flashing. It was as if the cavalry had shown up in the nick of time in a Western movie.

The angry crowd began to disperse with the women and children running for their homes. But the APD moved quickly and rounded up all the men who were trying to leave and began questioning each of them separately. A couple of ambulances arrived shortly after the police, and medics quickly began to evaluate the injured. They quickly began to treat Ginger, Vic, and Mr. Odom.

Tony's dad was able to get a few swings in before being overcome by the mob, but other than Mr. Race's broken nose and a couple of the mobsters sporting black eyes, no one was seriously injured. Now that the police had restored order, Tony and his mom walked out on the porch and watched as the police questioned Mr. Race, the dog owner, and the other men under the streetlight in front of Mr. Race's yard. They also watched with great concern as the medics tended to Ginger, Mr. Odom, and Vic who were standing in their yard quite a distance away from the stick-wielding, brick-throwing neighbors.

During the police interrogation, Tony could tell that the battle was over, but the war had just begun. The neighbors would shout, "Liar" whenever Vic or Mr. Odom were telling the medics their side of the story, and Vic and Ginger would reciprocate the same whenever one of the neighbors gave the police their side of the story. Amazingly, Vic's wounds, although painful, were not severe. They were mostly to his head and hands, so the medics wrapped a thick white gauze around his head several times and dressed the rest of the wounds with antiseptic and bandages. Mr. Odom received a few dressings for his head and face injuries as well as a lot of thanks from Vic and the rest of the family.

Fortunately for Ginger, the brick that struck her in the head was above her left eye and not deep enough to require stitches. She received a large bandage over her wound, although there was nothing the paramedics could do for the hair loss she experienced. After Vic and Mr. Odom had been attended to, the officers began to question them. Not being able to determine who was lying and who threw the first punch, the police arrested all the men and took them to jail.

After everyone had left, Tony and his sister got a flashlight and walked around in the yard, looking at the debris and blood left over from the fight. This once pristine yard was now littered with broken pieces of brick, broken sticks, and a piece of concrete cinder block.

"Will Dad have to spend the night in jail?" Tony asked his sister, who was proudly sporting the large bandage over her eye.

"I don't think so. Mom is fixing to go get him. She's gathering some paperwork that will get him released."

As the flashlight moved back and forth over the area where most of the fighting took place, the light illuminated several locks of dirty blond hair where Tony's sister had been assaulted. After seeing the aftermath of what was truly a horrific sight for the eight-year-old, he asked, "Can we go back inside now? I'm scared." Feeling anger for what happened and sadness for her little brother, Ginger took his hand, and they both walked up the eight cement steps and back into the house and locked the door.

After posting a property bond, Vic was back home by 11 o'clock. Mr. Odom also made bail that night and was back with his family around the same time. It was unknown how long Mr. Race stayed behind bars since no one seen him around his home for quite some time after the brawl.

Tony was already in bed when his dad returned home from the police station, but the traumatized little boy was too afraid to go to sleep. As he listened from his bedroom, he could tell his dad was still upset about the events that had transpired just hours earlier. He was still cussing the neighbors, threatening to get even, calling them all a bunch of liars, complaining they were trespassing on his property, how he had to go to court, and a lot of other words Tony was too young to understand. He heard his mom say something about moving, but she did not say when or where.

As Tony laid in bed staring at the stained pine wood ceiling and trying to block out the conversation between his parents, he thought of the violent scene he had just witnessed in his front yard. He also began to think about the fuzzy puppy, the rock that sent him to the hospital, and the black cat that he seen die under the same streetlight the neighbors and the police were standing under tonight. He had experienced a lot of traumatic events, and he could not get them out of his head.

What can I do to stop being scared? he thought as he held his pink rabbit and black and white dog up close to him. Tony thought about praying but was not sure if he remembered how. He had not prayed in some time and had never prayed for help. His prayers had mostly been about Christmas presents and things he wanted and not because he was scared. He prayed for a pony once and got upset when he looked in the backyard the next morning and it was not there.

To restore his faith in prayer, his mom explained that God couldn't give him a pony because a pony needed a lot of land and someone to care for it, and it might die if it lived in their backyard. The disappointed youngster accepted that it was not "God's will," and his faith was immediately restored.

"Jesus?" the nervous youngster said softly in a shaky but tearful voice.

Tony's mom had prayed with him a lot before they stopped going to church. They attended the First Baptist Church in Atlanta for a while, but every Sunday on the way home, his dad would cuss the preacher, the sermon, the people, and everything else he wasn't pleased with. After months of that, Tony's mom told him she wasn't going back since he wasn't happy there. They never looked for another church, and this disappointed Tony since he enjoyed going to Sunday school. Not long after they stopped going, she stopped praying with him, but she had taught him Jesus was always listening, and he would hear him pray when he called his name.

"Jesus, are you there? I need you to help me to not be scared."

Tony thought about the prayer his mom would have him repeat after her when she prayed with him at night. Even though he had not recited it in a long time, he was hoping he could still remember it. He began to whisper softly, believing Jesus would hear him even if he were whispering. "Now I lay me . . . down to sleep . . . I pray dear Lord . . . my soul you will keep . . . if I should die . . . before I wake . . . I pray dear Lord . . . my soul you will take . . . please Lord, help me not to be scared . . . Amen."

Having said his prayer, he felt at peace . . . safe . . . and sleepy. Tony rolled over, faced the wall, pulled his pillow over his head as he had often done to drown out the ugly words that were still coming from the living room, snuggled up to his stuffed animals, and then drifted off to sleep.

Several weeks passed without any verbal or physical confrontations with the neighbors. Most everyone kept to themselves and just ignored each other, being most of the men were out on bail and no one wanted to disturb the peace and wind up in jail. It seemed things had finally calmed down on Polar Rock Place, although you could feel the tension whenever any of the neighbors encountered Vic or any other family member in the driveway, at the mailbox, or on the street. Tony celebrated his ninth birthday in November that year with just a handful of family members. Thanksgiving, Christmas, and New Year's Day came for the StCyr family without any interruptions or disturbances.

Beginning to accept the fact that things would never get better in the neighborhood, Tony's parents decided to move to an apartment complex that did not allow pets and where there were no yards for Vic to tend to or dogs to crap in. They found the perfect place in Forest Park, and the family moved to Villa Capri Apartments. To be completely disconnected from Polar Rock Place, Vic knew he had to sell the red brick ranch. Knowing how his Southern-born neighbors felt about Black people, integration, and the civil rights movement that was in full swing in the mid-sixties, to fulfill his promise to get even, Vic listed his house with a Black-owned real estate company. This infuriated his neighbors, which was his intention. If he were alive today, he would still laugh and tell you, "Integrating the neighborhood was better than whipping their ass!"

The next time the family seen their neighbors was at court. Tony remembers taking the stand and giving his side of the story, but he does not remember much else. He just knew the judge ruled in his dad and Mr. Odom's favor.

After the hearing was over, Lester Maddox, Vic's attorney and soon-to-be governor of Georgia, told Tony, "You did good up there on that stand, son. Maybe you should become an attorney."

Tony smiled and answered, "Maybe I can." Then he asked, "What's an attorney?"

Tony and his mom in the front yard on Polar Rock Place.

CHAPTER X

BOMBS, BOTTLES, AND BOXING CHAMPION

The family, especially Tony, took to apartment living quite well. The young boy had a lot more pavement and asphalt to ride his bike on, and the speed breakers scattered throughout the complex made riding around the apartment buildings more fun and exciting. He loved using the speed bumps as ramps and seeing if he could navigate the tires of his high handle-barred, banana seat bicycle between the two yellow-striped asphalt humps without touching either of them as he raced up and down the interior roadways meeting neighbors and exploring the large complex that he now called home. He also had access to an Olympic size swimming pool during the summer, a fully equipped playground with the latest swings, merry-go-round and climbing bars, a convenience store near the entrance of the complex, and a new best friend named Larry.

There were no more fights among neighbors, no more killing animals, and no more vandalism. Apartment life was much calmer and less stressful than it was on Polar Rock place for the now ten-year-old, although the arguing and cussing between his mom and dad remained unchanged. The name-calling and verbal abuse Tony had experienced most of his life continued, although it seemed less frequent than before, possibly because he was outside more and only came home most days at supper time.

Tony's mom continued her pattern of leaving Vic, moving in with one of her sisters, and then returning home after a couple of weeks. On one of those separations when Tony was nine, he began to wonder if this was going to be a permanent move for them since the "D" word was beginning to come up more frequently in his mom's conversations with family and friends.

Instead of returning to Vic after a couple of weeks, she rented an apartment in Sylvan Hills, a government project off Sylvan Road in South Atlanta near the Lakewood Shopping Center where she now worked. She also enrolled Tony into a new school and bought new furniture. A man who Tony had never seen before kept hanging around his mom and even helped them move into the rundown apartment. After the furniture was in place, Tony's mom told him to go outside and play. He thought it was strange of his mom to ask him to go outside being he was still unpacking his toys and clothes, but since he had seen the large courtyard and the playground from the breezeway when they were moving in, he knew there were plenty of new things to explore, so he happily agreed. As he approached the open door, he hesitated since he was not familiar with his new surroundings and asked, "Are you coming with me, Mom?"

His mom responded, "Not right now, but I'll be watching you from the window." Her words reassured the nervous youngster, so he turned and headed out the door.

Directly behind their apartment building was a rectangular courtyard that was mostly dirt with some grass growing near the edge of the side-walk. There were six twenty-four-unit brick apartment buildings sur-rounding the dirty neglected courtyard; two of the apartment buildings were on one side with two on the opposite side and a sidewalk separating the buildings leading to similar courtyards and apartments. A single twen-ty-four-unit apartment building was situated 150 yards across the dusty courtyard opposite the apartment building Tony and his mom had just moved into.

Tony could tell when he entered the courtyard that this was not as nice as Villa Capri. The courtyard was littered with rusty clothesline poles, and the cracked and broken sidewalk that ran around the perim-eter looked more like an obstacle course than a place for the youngster to ride his bike. Worst of all . . . there was no swimming pool! He did get excited when he seen the unfenced playground in the distance, so he headed straight for it.

As he was investigating the rusty playground equipment, he looked up to make sure he was in sight of his mom, but instead of his mom looking out her bedroom window, he seen the strange man watching him. After they made eye contact, the man disappeared from the window, and Tony began to play. Since the playground consisted mostly of broken swings, a rusty merry-go-round, and weathered monkey bars, Tony got bored quickly, so he decided to do pull-ups on the rusty T-shaped clothes-line poles situated behind each apartment building.

When Tony came to the first pole, the short nine-year-old jumped up and grabbed it from the side, then pulled himself up to look through the opening like a pirate would look through a periscope. When Tony did not see any light on the other end, the youngster dropped back down to the ground, wondering why he was not able to see through to the other side. *That's never happened before*, the confused boy thought. *I've always been able to see through a clothesline pole.* He decided to take a second look to see if there was something blocking his view or if the pole was made differently than other poles he had encountered. When he jumped up and grabbed the pole the second time, the pole shook a little more violently than it had previously. When he pulled himself up and put his right eye over the hole, he noticed a small dark shadow moving in the dim light, but he could not make out what it was. Tony did not realize there was a large wasp nest near the opening that was blocking the young explorer's view.

Before Tony could figure out what the moving shadow was, he felt a sharp, excruciating pain he had never felt before! One of the angry red wasps had stung him above his eye. He let go of the pole, dropped to the ground, and ran as fast as he could to the new apartment, screaming from the pain. Since the apartment did not have air conditioning, all the windows to the second-floor unit were open, so his mom heard him screaming and crying as he ran across the courtyard. She was standing outside the door in the breezeway as the injured youngster ran up the metal steps toward her. She could see he was holding his hand over his right eye as he made his way up the stairs toward her. Having been stung on the hand by a yellow jacket when he put a small rock over the hole they were flying in and out of when he lived on Polar Rock Place, he knew what a bee sting felt like, but this sting was much worse than the yellow jacket and more painful than the rock that had sent him to the hospital. When Tony reached the top of the stairs, his mom asked frantically, "What happened, son?"

Since Tony had gotten a split-second glimpse of the wasp, he responded, "A red wasp stung me!"

Tony's mom hurried him into the apartment, made a cold compress, and applied it to his eye. After the pain subsided, she removed the dishrag and was relieved to see that the sting was on the eyelid and not directly on his eye. As his mom began to explain how lucky he was that the stinger had missed his eyeball, he noticed that her clothes were disheveled, and the strange man's shirt was off. She politely asked the man to leave, which he did.

Tony believes the wasp sting was God's way of interrupting something his mom was about to do that she may have regretted later. But just like previous times, Vic, not wanting to be a divorcee again, apologized to his mom for his bad behavior and vowed to be better to her and Tony. After only two weeks in the projects, Tony and his mom moved back in with his dad.

As hard as it was living with the abuse, Tony was relieved to be back with his dad at the Villa Capri apartments. He was especially thankful for the nice playground, swimming pool, asphalt, an air-conditioned home, and being back with his best friend Larry.

Tony and Larry were as close as two young boys could be. The thin brown-headed boy was a year older and slightly taller than Tony and had an outgoing personality that made him fun to be around. Tony and Larry were virtually inseparable. They rode bikes, played with cars in the dirt, hunted four-leaf clovers, played on the playground, went swimming, and occasionally spent the night at each other's apartment. If you saw one, you most likely saw the other. Tony had never had a best friend before. His cousin Marty was like a best friend, but they only seen each other occasionally on weekends and special holidays, so having someone to play and explore with daily was a welcome experience for Tony.

One of the favorite summer treats that each family seem to always have on hand were popsicles. Since nice toys were things rich kids had, each boy would save their popsicle sticks and use them to make their own playthings like darts, tiny shovels, car ramps, army men barricades, and fake knives. To make a wood knife or dart, the boys would rub both sides of one of the rounded edges at a slant on the sidewalk or brick building until it made the desired point they wanted.

One of the things they made from these sticks were what the boys called "stick bombs." Each boy would take five or six of the color-stained sticks, place them over each other, and then slide the ends over and under in a square or triangle shape, creating pressure points throughout the framework. When the sticks were thrown, and they hit an object, they would explode apart like a bomb. They threw these at each other's forts, army men, matchbox cars, and even each other.

One night they decided to throw their hand-crafted devices at moving cars. Tony's parents were gone to one of their many lodge functions, so Ginger was babysitting. Since she didn't want her little brother hearing her phone conversations, she let him stay out after dark, something his mom and dad would never let him do. They laid down in the grass near a main travel route through the apartment buildings, and as cars passed, they would throw their stick bombs at the tires. "Hitting a moving target is much more fun than hitting the Hot Wheels cars or army men," Larry said as he went into the street to collect the exploded popsicle sticks.

"Hurry, here comes another car!" Tony shouted from his position in the darkness only ten feet from the road. Larry hurried back and laid down on his stomach beside his friend as Tony readied another stick bomb. When the car approached, he threw it at the right rear tire, but instead of hitting the tire, his stick bomb hit the fender above the tire. It exploded on impact, making a louder than usual noise, but instead of the driver continuing down the road, he slammed on his brakes, opened the door, and jumped out to see what had hit his car. Tony and Larry buried their heads in the tall dew-soaked grass and laid motionless on their stomachs, hoping the man wouldn't see them. The angry man shouted into the darkness, "I don't know what you threw, but you better not do it again!" Then he got back in his car and drove off.

"That was close!" Larry said as he rolled over on his back, grabbed his stomach, and let out a sigh of relief.

"It sure was. I was scared to death!" Tony sighed as he rolled over on his back. "I threw it too high." As the youngsters stared into the starlit sky and talked about the driver, his new shiny car, and how close they came to being caught, Larry rolled back over on his elbows, looked at Tony, and said, "We better get out of here in case he comes back with a flashlight."

"I agree." The two boys picked up the evidence that was laying in the street, left the area, and never threw stick bombs at cars again . . . at least that's their story.

Tony attended J. E. Edmonds Elementary School in Forest Park for his third and fourth-grade years. It was during this time that he realized he was younger, smaller, and weaker than the other kids in his class, and he was unable to compete with the older, taller, and stronger boys in pull-ups, sit-ups, kickball, and other physical activities. This caused the older boys to bully him and the girls to pick on him. He complained to his parents, but his dad's advice was always, "Bust them in the nose," or "Kick them in the balls." Tony was not willing to do either, so he just tolerated the ill-usage and walked away. He believes seeing the fight that took place in his front yard turned him against violence, which further subjected him to mistreatment by the other children.

One warm summer day, when he was on the playground, a classmate who lived in the complex came over to where Tony was standing between the fence and the climbing bars with a couple of friends who also lived in the complex and started challenging Tony to a fight. Tony was minding his own business and did not know why the eleven-year-old classmate wanted to fight him. The boy started pushing Tony on the left shoulder with his right hand, saying, "Hit me. Come on, chicken, hit me!" Tony kept backing up, telling his classmate to leave him alone. He did not want to fight him, but the boy kept pushing Tony as he backed up toward the corner of the fence surrounding the playground.

The other two boys were bigger than Tony, Scott, who was twelve, and another boy, who was also eleven, were laughing and joined in the name-calling as Tony retreated. There is an old saying Tony's Aunt Alice told him growing up, "Never back a coward into a corner. He'll kill you!" Someone should have told these bullies that. When Tony's back touched the fence, all hell broke loose! It was as if every fear and emotion the youngster had been holding inside him all of his life exploded into adrenaline. The small-framed ten-year-old began swinging both his bony fists at the bully as hard and as fast as he could. He busted his lip, bloodied his nose, and hit the kid so many times so fast that he didn't have time to defend himself. His classmate took off running home, crying and screaming along the way. One of the other boys approached Tony as he was swinging his way out of the corner and said, "Don't you hit my . . ." Before he could finish his statement, Tony busted him in the nose and mouth a few times before he took off running. The other boy, Scott, who was two years older than Tony and much bigger, stepped in front of Tony with his fists raised and said, "You don't hurt my fr . . ." But Tony wasn't listening . . . he was swinging. He busted the twelve-year-old in the mouth and bloodied his nose and sent him running out of the playground, heading toward home, crying like a baby.

When it was all over, Tony had beat up the three bullies and had not received a scratch. When the excitement was over, Tony stood frozen, wondering how he was able to fend off the three attackers who were older and stronger than him. He snapped out of it when he heard the other kids on the playground who apparently had been bullied by these boys clapping and saying things like, "That'll teach them to leave you alone," or "Way to go, Tony. Didn't know you had it in you!"

Tony stood for a moment, not really realizing if he was going to be in trouble or not, so he took off running toward home, doing a little crying himself. When he entered the front door, his mom, his dad, and Ginger quickly stood up and began asking the sobbing youngster what was wrong.

Through his tears, he began trying to tell them, "I (sniff), I (sniff), I beat up three boys on the playground!"

"You did what?" his mom asked frantically.

"Atta boy!" his dad shouted as he began inspecting his son for cuts and bruises. After looking him over, he said, "I don't see any blood, and you look okay."

Ginger asked curiously, "What happened?"

After Tony explained everything, his dad said, "Why are you crying then? You won!"

"Am I in trouble?" Tony said wiping his nose with the tissue his mom had given him.

The rest of the family started laughing, and his dad replied, "No, you're not in trouble. You did great!"

"And you won't ever be in trouble when you defend yourself!" his mom added.

Tony walked back to the playground with a newfound confidence and with his head held high. As Tony entered the gate, his best friend Larry began slapping him on the back as other kids who seen the fight walked over and thanked him for, in their words, "Giving them punks what they deserved!"

Scott lived in the apartment building that overlooked the swimming pool and playground. As Tony was being congratulated, he looked up and seen the twelve-year-old leaning over the concrete wall of the second-floor breezeway with a rag over his fat lip. He had heard what the other kids were saying, so he shouted out, "It was a lucky hit, that's all!"

The other kids began to chide back, "If it was a lucky hit, then come on back down here and fight him again!" And another said, "It was three on one; you deserved it!" One of the older boys said, "He don't have his friends now, so he's scared!" A few other insulting jabs were aimed at the thick-lipped pre-teen, including, "Who's the chicken now, huh?" and "Need some lipstick?"

Larry, who was the same size as Scott, put his thumbs under his armpits and looked up at the unrepentant bully, flapping his elbows while walking like a chicken, saying, "Bwak, bwak, bwak, bwaaaak!" The rest of the children laughed.

Tony appreciated the support he was receiving from the other children and the taunting of the humiliated bully, but he was wishing they would hush because he didn't want to fight Scott again or anyone else for that matter! *Three fights in one day is enough!* he thought. *Besides, I might get hit next time, and I don't like pain.*

After hearing enough taunts and insults, Scott turned around and carried his bloody rag, arrogance, and fat lip back to his apartment. When everyone seen that Scott had retreated, the excitement abated, and things returned to normal on the small playground.

The days and weeks following were different for the ten-year-old. He walked and rode his bike around the apartment complex with a confidence and respect he had never felt before. His best friend Larry had been spreading the news to the neighborhood kids how his best friend whooped three bullies on the playground. Though Tony was happy for the compliments, he was not sure if he wanted everyone to know about the fight in case someone wanted to try to unseat the new "Playground Champion." But after no one offered to fight him, he decided being feared around the complex was much better than being picked on.

Larry educated Tony on the art of "bottle picking." His best friend told him he could get three cents for every soda bottle he collected. All he had to do was clean them up and turn them in to the convenience store located at the front of the complex. Since Tony didn't get an allowance or other luxuries like candy bars and soft drinks very often, this intrigued Tony. While other kids were playing or swimming, Tony spent much of his free time looking for these redeemable cash commodities. After school, during summer vacation, and on weekends you would see the hard-working boy riding his bike around the complex, digging through trash cans, looking in ditches, and even riding alongside dangerous nearby roadways looking for bottles.

Tony learned real quick which neighbors drank Coke, Pepsi, Dr. Pepper, RC, and other brands, and which trash cans had bottles and which ones didn't. He also learned that people threw bottles at road signs from their car windows, so he would always find a cache of bottles near the traffic signs, although some would be cracked or broken. When one-liter Cokes came, out the hunt was on! Each one-liter Coke bottle was worth five cents, nearly twice the value of six and twelve-ounce bottles. Finding a one-liter bottle excited Tony as much as a gold nugget excited a prospector.

Occasionally, the eager lad would knock on doors in the complex and ask residents if they had any bottles they wanted to throw away. Many of the residents gladly gave the young entrepreneur soda bottles and insisted he come back every week. Sometimes a resident would give him a six-pack, which was like hitting the jackpot for the bottle collector.

Once the basket on the front of his bicycle was full, Tony would head to the Tenneco convenient store gas station with his bounty. There he would exchange the trash for cash and then buy whatever his heart desired, which usually included his favorite soft drink, a candy bar, and a pack of baseball cards that contained a piece of bubble gum as a bonus.

Collecting bottles, trading them for cash, and getting to enjoy the fruit of his labor gave the youngster a feeling of success, accomplishment, and pride. It also gave him some much-needed momentary escapes from the arguing, cussing, and verbal abuse he often experienced at home. When the succulent taste of a 3 Musketeers bar mixing with the fizzy ice-cold Pepsi Cola from a glass bottle reached his taste buds, and while reading the latest stats of his favorite baseball players on the back of their card, Tony often thought, *This must be how rich kids must live every day!*

Not long after Larry had shown Tony the art of bottle collecting, he moved from Villa Capri, and Tony never seen or heard from him again. Tony never had a friend as close as Larry and never had one afterward. Larry still crosses Tony's mind occasionally. He had hoped their paths would cross again one day, but being Tony could never remember his best friend's last name, he gave up hope. He still cherishes the great times they had together in Villa Capri Apartments. After the tumultuous years on Polar Rock Place, the time spent with Larry was like heaven on earth. It was truly the best two and a half years of Tony's childhood.

A few months after Larry moved, the StCyr family moved to Amulet Villas, a newly built town home community less than two miles from Villa Capri. The two-bedroom, two-story townhome was much nicer than the apartment. It had carpet in the bedrooms, on the stairs, and in the living room. There was a full bathroom upstairs with a half-bath downstairs, and the kitchen was equipped with the latest appliances, including a dishwasher, something his mom greatly appreciated since she had never owned one.

There was a church across the street with a large parking lot where Tony could ride his bicycle and fly his kite, and there was a pond behind the complex for tenants and their guests to fish in. There was a swimming pool near the back entrance, but there was no playground. Tony doesn't remember swimming in the pool, but he does remember spending countless hours at the pond catching tadpoles, skipping rocks, fishing, catching turtles (he got bit on the thumb once by a snapping turtle), shooting at dragonflies with his slingshot (he actually hit one in midflight), and walking across the frozen pond one winter watching the water move under the ice, wondering what he would do if he fell through (he never told his parents about that stupid stunt).

Tony also learned from some of the tenants how to catch bass with live salamanders and catfish with canned dog food. The pond at Amulet Villas was better than the playground at Villa Capri. It was Tony's go-to place when he needed to escape the harsh words, the constant fighting, and to just . . . be alone.

There were lots of things for an adventurous child to do around the townhomes, but there was no best friend, no memory of the fight that made him the playground champion, and no convenient store nearby. Since his ability to earn extra money by selling bottles came to a halt, he could no longer treat himself to an ice-cold Pepsi, a 3 Musketeers, or the latest pack of Topps baseball cards.

The move brought many disappointments, but Tony adjusted quickly. He also faced new challenges, including a new school, new friends, and a new way of life. But little did Tony know that it would only be for a short time because a totally unsuspecting and tragic event that would change his life forever was on the horizon.

Tony with a catfish from the pond behind Amulet Villas on Hendrix Drive in Forest Park. Behind him is his bottle collecting bicycle and the work truck his dad killed the puppy under.

Christmas at Amulet Villa. Tony loved that racetrack almost as much as his bicycle. His mom always gave him a Life Saver book at Christmas.

CHAPTER XI

THE KICK HEARD 'ROUND THE WORLD

H is dad was startled to see Tony coming down the stairs and immediately asked him why he wasn't at school. When Tony reached the bottom of the stairs, he explained that he hadn't felt good that morning, and Mom told him to stay home.

"I started feeling better about an hour ago when Mom called to check on me, and I asked if I could go fishing," Tony explained. "She said it'd be okay, so I was going to eat something and go to the pond."

His dad immediately began screaming and cussing at him, telling him if he was too sick to go to school, he was too sick to go fishing!

"Get your ass back up those stairs and back in the bed! You're not going anywhere!" Vic said angrily.

Tony wasn't sure what the big deal was, as he had permission from his mom, so he hesitated briefly, then turned to go back up the stairs as his dad had ordered. As his right foot touched the first step, his dad kicked him in the leg with his steel-toed shoe as hard as he could. He was trying to kick him in the buttocks, but since Tony was twelve now and taller than his dad, his foot didn't reach high enough, so the blow landed on the inner thigh of Tony's right leg. Tony fell forward onto the stairs. He had never in his life felt so much pain. He scrambled as fast as he could to get back up, and as he started to go up the stairs again, he looked over his shoulder just as his dad tried to kick him a second time. Fortunately, he missed. Tony hurried up the stairs, entered his bedroom, and shut the door. He fell on his bed, crying uncontrollably and in severe pain!

As Tony was lying on his bed, looking out his bedroom window, trying to figure out what had just happened and why, he felt a throbbing in the area where he was kicked. He pulled his pants down and seen a large welt forming on the inside of his right thigh. The thin polyester pants didn't do much to protect the tender skin from the steel-toed shoe. The wound was a deep shade of purple, and since it wasn't bleeding, it was swelling fast. All Tony could do was lay there sobbing, hoping his dad would hurry and leave so he could get something to eat and put some ice over his wound to ease the pain.

After about ten minutes, his dad called him back downstairs. Tony was scared and shaking as he descended slowly down the staircase, not knowing what to expect once he reached the bottom. He now had a limp, but he didn't dare let his dad see him limp. When he reached the bottom of the stairs, he saw his dad seated at the kitchen table.

"Com' here and sit down!" his dad said harshly. Then he pushed the bologna and mayonnaise toward him and said, "Fix you something to eat."

As Tony was fixing a sandwich, his dad offered a halfhearted apology for kicking him.

Then he threatened him, "If you tell your mother what just happened, it'll be worse next time!"

Tony looked up at his dad and responded with a short, confirming nod.

"After you finish eating and clean up your mess, you can go fishing." Then he left and went back to work.

On the way to the pond, Tony was hurting so bad that it was hard to walk. He knew he had to tell his mom. He might need medical attention since the wound seemed to be swelling by the minute. But how would his dad react if he told her? Would he hit her? Kick him again? He was already afraid of his dad, and now because of this incident and his threatening comment, his fear has taken on a whole new level.

Tony didn't fish long. He couldn't. His mind wasn't on it. He was hurting, not just hurting from the pain of the kick but also hurting from the fact that his dad had crossed the line from discipline and verbal abuse into battery.

This can't be good, he thought as he struggled to make the quarter-mile walk back up the hill to his home. His limp is more pronounced now that the welt is larger and rubbing against the inside of his pants. The pain is becoming more severe with each step. He began second-guessing if he should tell his mom or not. He kept wondering how this would affect his already-strained relationship with his dad. He was also wondering what impact it would have on his parents' relationship if he told his mom.

"Mom has left Dad in the past for a lot less," he said aloud as he rehearsed in his mind all the ways this might play out.

"We'll move in with Aunt Alice or Aunt Barbara," he thought as he remembered the last few times they separated.

"I'll have to change schools . . . again!" Tony hated changing schools. He had already attended five different schools in six years.

"How long will they be separated this time?" he mumbled. "A month, three months? Dad will apologize, they'll make up, and we'll be right back here in the same mess in a few weeks . . ."

By the time Tony reached to put his key in the door, he had decided that he wasn't going to tell his mom what his dad had done. If she found out another way that would be okay, but he wasn't going to say anything. He liked living near a pond, he didn't want to change schools again, he liked flying his kite and riding his bike in the church parking lot, he liked his friends in the apartment complex, and he had a nice room and a nice bed. Yes, he was hurting . . . but life wasn't all bad . . . at least not yet.

Things were normal at the supper table that night. Tony's leg was still throbbing and swollen, but he had changed to a loose pair of pants so it wouldn't hurt when he walked. Since it was Friday night, Tony's dad hurried off to a lodge meeting after supper, leaving him and his mom alone. Tony got up from the table and grimaced as he grabbed the back of his leg.

"What's the matter?" His mom seen the pain on her young son's face.

Tony was in a predicament. He had never lied to his mom before, but he didn't want to tell her what happened. As he stood motionless, holding his leg, and trying to decide what to say, he busted out crying and hollered, "Dad kicked me!"

Tony shuttered as he pushed the thoughts he had just relived from his mind. The pain, horror, and fear brought him back to the new house, his playroom, and . . . Gilligan's Island. For the first time since Tony could remember, he was finally at peace in his home. There was no one screaming, no fighting, no fear, and no one calling him ugly names.

With his mom at work and him home alone with his own television, he could finally have some peace and quiet, some r and r, and . . . an after-school nap. He could finally relax. He had finally found some freedom and independence. But he would soon learn that this newfound freedom and independence would come with a heavy price.

The house on Rambling Road in Kennesaw as it was in 1971.

CHAPTER XII

A DREAM OF FIELDS FULFILLED

By the time Tony and his mom had finished moving to Kennesaw, baseball signups had already begun. The first Saturday after they were settled in, Tony had his mom at the baseball field filling out paperwork. His mom didn't have the money to pay the registration fees, but Tony didn't know that. After renting a moving truck and paying the utility deposits and other moving expenses, she had just enough money left for gas and a few groceries. But she also knew how much her son wanted to play baseball, and she didn't want to disappoint him, especially after everything he had been through.

As she was about to write the check, she looked over and observed her son doing something she hadn't seen him do in a long time. He was laughing. Yes, laughing out loud. He was full of excitement, happiness, and joy, something neither one of them had felt in a long time. He was talking to other players and throwing a ball into his glove repeatedly as he shared a few of his "backyard baseball war stories" as he called them.

His favorite baseball war story came about when they were living in Amulet Villas. He was only eleven, but he was playing ball with some of the older kids when he missed a line drive hit right at him that tipped the top of his glove and hit him square in his left eye. Since the baseball was waterlogged, it was heavier than normal, so it fractured his eye socket and caused a lot of bruising and swelling. His eye was swollen for weeks. It was so swollen that he could look across the bridge of his nose and see his eyelashes.

He's probably telling that story, she thought as she watched him interacting with the other players who were also there for signups.

Lately, she had been second-guessing herself on her decision to leave Vic and was concerned about the impact the divorce would have on her young son. But based on her observation today, there seems to be no need for concern. Watching him laugh and smile and filled with excitement was a part of him that she had never seen before. It was as if he had emerged from a cocoon as a new person. And she liked this new person.

Maybe getting a divorce was the right thing? she thought as she rested her head in her hand, admiring her new son.

Tony turned and made eye contact with his mom. She smiled, and he smiled back, then he returned to the conversation with his new friends.

"Ma'am, do you have any questions?" the rec department worker asked softly.

Tony's mom startled, sat straight up, and replied, "Uh, no . . . uh, yes ma'am . . . who do I make this check out to?"

"CCPR is fine," the worker replied.

Tony's mom finished filling out the check, tore it from the checkbook, and handed it to the rec department worker.

"Here's a list of all the things your son will need by opening day. Tryouts are in two weeks. Looks like you're all set."

Tony's mom rose and said, "Thank you so much."

The lady replied, "You're very welcome!"

Tony would learn later that his mom made a huge sacrifice for him that year.

On the short drive home, Tony was looking over the list of items he needed while his mom was trying to figure out how she was going to come up with the money to buy them all.

"I have most of these items already," Tony broke the silence.

"You do?" Tony's mom asked with a sigh of relief.

"Yes ma'am. The only thing I need is cleats and a cup with a jock strap, whatever that is."

Tony's mom was chuckling. "You don't know what a jock strap and cup is?"

"Nope! Never needed one, I guess. What is it?"

Tony's mom was wishing his dad had explained this to him when he was younger. "It's what athletes use to cover their privates with so if they get hit with a ball, it doesn't hurt as bad. Thankfully, those things aren't that expensive. When I get paid next weekend, we'll go shopping."

Tony was in shock! He knew what it felt like to be hit there. It happened to him several times when he was wrestling with his cousins but never with a baseball. He thought of his eye and how it swelled and how horrible it would be to be hit there and have those things swell like his eye did.

"Ouch!" he thought aloud as he envisioned his testicles swollen like his eye.

He wanted to ask more questions, but he didn't want to ask his mom. *That would be embarrassing,* he thought as the car turned into the subdivision. He had never seen a cup before, so in his mind, he's thinking of a Tupperware cup like he drank tea out of. Was he in for a surprise? He decided he would think about his new cleats instead. He had never owned cleats before. He was excited!

"It says here I can have metal or rubber cleats," Tony broke the silence.

"I'll have to buy you what I can afford. This new house has set me back a bit," Tony's mom responded.

"I understand. I don't really care as long as I can play baseball!" Tony said very enthusiastically.

His mom looked at her very happy son, who was tossing the baseball into his glove again but with less force. She smiled as they pulled into the driveway of their new home. It wasn't very big, but it was new, and it was a home, a home without fussing and cussing, and most of all, no fighting! It was up a hill in a cul-de-sac, so there was very little traffic that came up the street. It was approximately 1,000 square feet with a carport and cement drive. It didn't have much furniture, but it did have a kitchen table with mismatched chairs, a rocking chair in the living room, and inexpensive bedroom furniture for each of their bedrooms. There was a playroom with a small black and white television, Tony's portable record player he had gotten as a Christmas gift a few years earlier, and a soft, comfortable chair. The yard was small but bordered a large tract of tall pines and hard woods that gave Tony a place to go exploring.

Having lived in apartments since he was nine, he welcomed the nearby forest. Since the subdivision was new, there were houses under construction nearby and an empty lot to the right of their home. The house payment with insurance was ninety-eight dollars per month, a lot less than the apartments his parents had been renting. Tony knew how much his mother made and felt confident that the ninety-eight-dollar house payment was very affordable. He felt like this might be their forever home. Life was finally looking up for Tony. He was happy, excited, and feeling confident about his future. And then . . . there was Tigger.

Since Vic wouldn't let Tony have a dog, he wanted a dog nearly as bad as he wanted to play baseball. Shortly after Vic and his mom separated and within weeks of moving in with his Aunt Alice, Tony had a beautiful miniature collie that he named Tigger. He named his new best friend Tigger after the story book character from Winnie the Pooh because he liked the character, and because he was "the only one" dog that Tony had ever had. Since his Aunt Alice had a fenced backyard, Tigger had a lot of room to run and play in, so it worked out perfectly for Tony.

Tigger stayed at his aunt's house while their house was being built, but now that they've settled into their new home, Tigger is with Tony once again, although he's not too fond of the leash he's on after running free for months. This would prove to be a problem.

By the next Saturday, Tony's mom had come up with the money to buy the rest of the things he needed, cleats, a jock strap, and a cup. They went to a local sporting goods store in Cartersville to purchase everything. Buying cleats with his mom present wasn't an issue. The store had plenty of steel and rubber cleats in stock, but Tony took the least expensive rubber pair. Buying the jock strap wasn't an issue either.

It was hanging on a peg where it was easily accessible, and there was a size chart available that matched a player's underwear size with the jock straps. But buying the cup wasn't as easy. They couldn't find any on the floor. They walked and walked, looking for cups.

Why couldn't these things be with the jock straps? I don't even know what I'm looking for! he thought as he wandered around the store.

Walking around with his mom and looking for something for his privates was embarrassing enough. Tony had never had to buy a jock strap or cup before, a sign to both of them that he was entering into manhood. Tony's mom finally asked a clerk where the cups were. As fate would have it, the store kept them behind the counter.

When Tony and his mom walked up to the counter, his mom said, "He needs a cup." She knew her son was embarrassed, so she was snickering. At that moment, Tony wanted to crawl under the carpet. He was wishing he was buying this with an uncle, a Marine, or some other man from another planet, just not his mom! He was so embarrassed. But he knew if he was going to play baseball, he would have to deal with this embarrassment.

Okay, Mom asked! It's over! he thought. "He'll reach under the counter . . . give me a cup, and . . . we'll be on our way.

"What size? Small, medium, or large?" the clerk asked, chuckling.

NO! That's not the way this is supposed to go! Tony thought to himself as the clerk and his mom are watching him turn a darker shade of red! "No one said anything about picking a size. Do you have a chart? Measuring tape? I have no clue!" he said all these things to himself as he was looking at their silly grins.

Without thinking, Tony shouted, "Large!"

The clerk and his mom both looked at him as if to say, "Are you sure about that?" But the embarrassed thirteen-year-old wasn't about to change his mind. He didn't know what a cup was until a few days ago, much less what sizes they came in. He just wanted to make sure "small" didn't come out of his mouth and be further embarrassed in front of his mom.

"Are you sure because you can't exchange these once they've been purchased?" The clerk asked.

"Yes, I'm sure!" Tony responded confidently.

His mom handed the clerk the money as they both had one final laugh at Tony's expense.

When they hopped back in the car, his mom asked him jokingly, "Well son, how does it feel to be a man now?"

Tony looked up at his mom, and seeing the smirky grin she was displaying, he put his chin in his hand, leaned forward, placed his elbow on his leg, and said, "Embarrassing!"

Tryouts went great for Tony. Even though he had missed seven years of competitive ball, he had become a decent baseball player. He was picked up by the Yankees, a fourteen-and-under team in Cobb County. The park was right off Highway 5, about a mile from his new home. Since Tony's mom worked a lot, Tony had to walk along the busy two-lane highway to and from practice. The coach had practice at the park at least three days a week, including Saturdays.

After walking to the park a few times, Tony decided he'd try hitchhiking. Tony didn't mind hitchhiking. His older cousins did it, other people did it, there was a song on the radio promoting it, and people on TV and in movies were doing it, so he didn't feel like it was dangerous. The thirteen-year-old would walk the quarter-mile distance from his home to the highway, turn right, and start walking in the direction of the park.

To make his bat and glove easier to carry, Tony would slide the knob of his wooden bat through the wrist strap of his glove and push it up on the barrel as far as it would go until it was secured in place. He would walk proudly along the side of the highway with his bat resting on his shoulder, much like a hunter or soldier carried a gun. The glove was raised high in the air much like a flag or banner at the end of a pole, signaling to every passing vehicle that this young ball player had a purpose and a mission. When a car or truck would approach, Tony would turn and face the vehicle and start walking backward with his thumb out just like he had seen other people do.

To Tony's surprise, many willing strangers would pick him up and carry the young, determined ball player to his destination. Thankfully, everyone who picked Tony up was of good moral character, although there was one shady person who gave him a ride who he wasn't completely sure about.

Since there was a convenience store near the park, Tony would often run in and buy enough bubble gum to supply all his teammates. Even though Tony's mom didn't have extra money to give him, he seemed to always have money. It wasn't a lot of money, but he had money. Even when he couldn't pick up bottles, he found a way to generate a small income. He learned the art of supply and demand while living at Amulet Villa.

When he was in sixth grade at Hendrix Drive Elementary, Batman was a very popular TV show. One day, Tony's dad brought home a case of Batman stickers that someone from a job site was throwing away. Each pack of stickers contained twelve bat-shaped stickers that were six inches wide and three inches tall, and written on each sticker was one of the words that appeared on the TV screen during the fight scenes like, "KAPOW," "SPLATT," "ZOWIE," and others. Tony decorated his notebook with these stickers, which was a common practice among students his age then. When he went back to school, his classmates asked him where he got them. Being that Tony was mostly ignored at school, this attention made him feel important and significant. Tony didn't reveal the source of his stickers but told his classmates he had more at home, and he would let them buy some if they would like.

The following day, Tony brought several packs to school and sold them for a dime each. It wasn't long before word got out to other classes that Tony had Batman stickers. Seeing how much in demand the stickers were, he raised his price to fifteen cents per pack. School kids in other grades were meeting him before and after school, buying his Batman stickers.

By the time Tony sold out, he was getting twenty-five cents per pack and had learned a valuable lesson in commerce not many children his age had learned. And since he had sold nearly one hundred packs of stickers, he also had a piggy bank full of money something many sixth graders didn't have. A few days after Tony had sold out of stickers and after finishing last in a foot race, his importance and significance waned, and things returned to normal for the young entrepreneur.

When he started attending his new school in Kennesaw, he learned quickly that footlong Big Buddy bubble gum sticks were in high demand at JJ Daniels Junior High. With a dime Tony had left over from lunch money, he bought two Big Buddy bubble gum sticks and took them to school the next day and sold them both for ten cents each. He went back to the store and bought four more sticks and sold them as well. As supply and demand increased, he raised his price to fifteen cents.

During the summer, he would dig through garbage cans, trash piles, and ride his bike up and down highways, collecting soft drink bottles so he could cash them in at grocery and convenient stores. Sometimes when Tony needed money, he would go to a junkyard near his home and rummage through the junk cars, looking in the ashtrays, glove boxes and even pulling the back seats out, looking behind them for change. He knew his mom didn't have money to give him, so he didn't ask. He would rake leaves during the fall or do odd jobs for neighbors.

One summer when he was twelve, he worked digging footings and pouring cement. This is how he made money and is how he bought soft drinks, candy bars, or a pen for school. This is how he survived without an allowance, and this is how he blessed his teammates with bubble gum!

After giving his team bubble gum for several weeks, he was hoping they would nickname him "Bubblegum." He never had a nickname other than Tony, which was short for Anthony, but he knew baseball players had nicknames, and now that he was a baseball player, he was hoping his nickname would be Bubblegum. It was silly, but he had seen a TV commercial where a kid playing baseball was called Bubblegum, and he liked the name. He often gave hints to his teammates as he handed them a piece of bubblegum, but they never picked up on it, so he was stuck being called Tony.

Most of the time, his mom was there to pick him up after practice. She knew that if she wasn't there, her son would have to walk the busy highway home or hitch a ride, which she knew both were dangerous. But she also knew that was the only way her son could get to practice and back home, something she hadn't considered when filing the divorce papers. On occasion, when she picked Tony up, if she made extra tips, she would treat her hardworking ball player to Jack's Burger Restaurant not far from the ball field. Tony loved it! They rarely ate out when she was married to Vic, so eating a fresh grilled hamburger with fries and a shake in a fast-food restaurant was a special treat. If she didn't make it to the park in time to pick him up or if practice was on Saturday, he would just walk or hitch hike home. He felt like the exercise helped him stay in shape.

One day after practice, the coach saw his mom wasn't there to get him, so he offered to take Tony home. After the one-mile drive to Tony's house, the coach asked him how he got to and from practice. Tony said he walked or hitchhiked. The coach immediately voiced his opposition and told him how dangerous walking along side that highway was, and if he didn't have a ride to the field, to call him, and he would pick him up. He also told him he would take him home if his mom couldn't. Since the coach's son was the best player on the team, and he and Tony had become friends, he liked that idea. He would just have to find another way to get his bubble gum.

It was opening day! Tony had waited for years for this opportunity, and he was determined to enjoy every minute of it. As he stood in right field, he realized he was on a team that mattered. Both the infield and outfield were covered with lush green grass that was soft like carpet beneath his newly purchased, off-brand rubber cleats. The base paths, the pitcher's mound, and the area outside the foul lines in front of the dugouts were smooth and manicured. The chalk that ran to the foul poles and outlined the batter's box looked like baby powder, and the snow-white bases positioned around the infield were like marshmallows floating on top of a cup of rich hot chocolate.

Instead of blue jeans and a t-shirt with Little League printed on them like he wore in Hapeville, Tony was wearing a white uniform with black pinstripes and was sporting a hat and vest with the official New York Yankees logo embroidered on them. Tony had never experienced anything like this before. He couldn't have been any happier than a rookie ball player that had just stepped on to a major league field. He was going to make the best of it because he didn't know if or when this experience would end. And make the best of it he did!

He took a deep breath as he waited for the game to start. He was wishing his mom could have been there to enjoy it with him, but with her managerial responsibilities, she had to work most Saturdays.

She'll make some of the night games, Tony thought. But he wasn't about to let her absence interfere with this moment. This was his moment, his time, so as the first pitch was thrown, he got in his ready position and focused on the game.

Tony has several memories of his season with the Yankees. One of his favorite memories happened in the aforementioned opening day game. He caught a fly ball in right field and threw a runner out at home trying to tag up and score from third base. It was an inning ending double play! The coach was very impressed with his new right field-er's throwing arm, and so was the other coach. He didn't try that again!

After only a few games, the coach found out that Tony could catch, so he became the starting catcher, quite a step up from the right field position where he started. He enjoyed catching. Even though Tony had only caught his cousin Marty in the backyard, he was still a better catcher than the one on his team. After a few games behind the plate, Tony learned quickly how important that cup was, although he wished he had opted for the medium.

Since Tony was a decent hitter, he batted in the middle of the lineup most of the season. He had never played any games at night, so playing games under the lights was something special for Tony, and he truly enjoyed it. He felt like he played better when the lights came on, some-thing he can't explain, and something many young ball players take for granted now. One of those games under the lights is embedded in his memory for ever.

They were playing the Tigers, one of the better fourteen-and-under teams in the league. It was the bottom of the inning and the Yankees last at-bat. The bases were loaded as Tony walked toward the plate. He looked at his coach for the sign, then stepped in the batter's box. His team was down three to zero.

Tony doesn't remember the sign, the count, or how many outs there were; he just remembers swinging and hitting a looping line drive to right field that went past the outfielder and rolled all the way to the fence. By the time the fielder had recovered the ball and threw it to his cutoff man, three runs had scored, and Tony was standing on third base. His teammates, the coaches, and the parents in the bleachers were standing, jumping, and hollering. It was Tony's only triple of his short baseball career, and it couldn't have come at a better time. The next batter drove Tony in, and the Yankees won four to three.

For the first time in Tony's life, he was a baseball hero. He had driven in three runs and scored the winning run. His teammates surrounded him as he crossed home plate, jumping and slapping him on the helmet. Parents were cheering, and coaches were giving him five as the team lined up to shake hands with their defeated and distraught opponents.

"Great game guys!" The coach said enthusiastically as Tony and his team-mates took a knee in a semi-circle facing the coach on the soft outfield grass. "That was an incredible come-back win and a heck of a team effort." The coach paused as he looked around at all his players. "But there's no doubt as to who deserves the game ball tonight!" Tony's heart began racing as he felt the excitement building. *Could it be me? Or is it the kid that drove me in? It must be one of us.* The coach looked directly at Tony, smiled and said, "Tony, you had heck of a game. You drove in three runs and scored the winning run." The coach tossed the ball to Tony and said, "Congratulations! You came through when we needed you to. Good game behind the plate too."

The coach gave a few more post-game instructions to everyone, but Tony wasn't listening. He was staring at the ball. He was examining the raised stitching, the threads, the scuff marks, the leather. He kept turning it over and over in his hand thinking, *Wow, my first game ball.*

Out of all the games their team played that year, that's the only score he can remember. But to Tony, that's the only one that mattered. It was the first time in his life that he felt such admiration, appreciation, and value. It was a great feeling, and he wanted his children to experience it. And he worked hard to make sure they did.

After that season, Tony realized that the talent pool was too good for him to be a serious competitor at a higher level. He had missed too many years of competitive baseball, and he knew he would never play high school ball or attend college, so he quit. But he did quit on a high note, and he has a lot of great memories of his team, the bubble gum, hitchhiking, the rides, his coach, and his time on the 14U Kennesaw Yankees.

Not long after baseball season ended, Tony was watching television in his playroom when his mom walked up, stood in the doorway, and said, "Turn the TV off, son. We need to talk."

Tony had heard that tone before, so he knew his mom had something important to talk about, so he got up, turned the TV off, sat back down, and asked nervously, "Am I in trouble?"

His mom laughed and said, "No silly, you're not in trouble."

Tony was relieved but asked nervously, "What's going on?"

"Well, I've been talking to your father over the past few weeks, and he wants us to get back together as a family. I told him I would talk to you and see what you thought. It's been almost a year, and his apologies seem really sincere this time, and I know he hurt you really bad, and he's truly sorry about that and says he'll never lay a hand on you again . . ." His mom paused when she saw the surprised look on her son's face. She looked down at the floor, looked back up at Tony, then leaned on the door jam, folded her arms, and asked concerningly, "What . . . what do you think?"

Tony wasn't sure what to think. He was shocked that his mom would even entertain the idea of re-marrying his dad and moving back in with him, especially after all he and his mom had been through. Tony answered emphatically and without hesitation, "You can move back in with him if you want, but I'll move in with Aunt Betty or Aunt Barbara. I'll be fourteen soon, and I can choose who I want to live with, but I am not moving back in with ya'll if you get back together."

Tony could tell this was not the answer his mom was hoping for. She had become lonely, and Tony was too young to understand that. He had heard her crying in her bedroom many nights over the past several months, so he knew she was taking being alone pretty hard. But he was not about to let her talk him into moving back under the same roof with the man who had kicked him like a dog and threatened to do worse if he told his mom.

As the two stared at each other, not knowing what to say, his mom asked softly, "Are . . . you sure . . . you won't reconsider?"

Tony looked around at his playroom and thought of the peace and tranquility he had been enjoying since moving into the new house. Then he thought of how many times he had heard the previous promises to "do better" his dad had made and how it only lasted for a while. Then he answered in the same manner, "No ma'am, I can't do it. I can go live with Betty or Barbara if you want to go back to Dad, but I just know ya'll would separate again." Tony paused, then asked, "What about the car, the house, and your new job?"

"I can sell the house, but your dad said I can keep the car. I would transfer to Greenbrier Mall and work as a manager there. He's not a bad man, I made mistakes too, plus . . ."

Tony's mom continued to make her argument for a few more minutes, but she could tell her words were falling on deaf ears, and her son wasn't budging, so she surrendered. As she slowly turned and retreated from the doorway, Tony got up, turned the television back on, adjusted the antennae, and sat back down in his soft chair. He wondered if he was being too stubborn and if he had made the right decision. *Am I being selfish?* he thought. *Am I thinking only of myself? Should I give Dad another chance for mom's sake?* While Tony stared through the black and white television, he wrestled with his thoughts and emotions. He wasn't sure if he had made the right decision. He was wishing his mom would've talked about it a little more. Finally, being content that he had made the correct decision, he pushed the thoughts out of his mind and began to laugh at the antics of the Beverly Hillbillies.

But in the kitchen, his mom wasn't laughing. She was crying quietly, making sure Tony didn't hear her. She was torn between remarrying her ex-husband and losing her son or keeping her son and remaining a divorcee. After doing some wrestling of her own, she chose to keep her son. If she had only knew how devastating her decision would be on both her and Tony, she may not have surrendered so easily!

Tony's first dog Tigger playing with Ricky House.

Tony in his 14U West Cobb Yankees uniform.

Tony and his 6th grade class. He was still smaller than most of the girls.

CHAPTER XIII
Liquor, Lust, & Losing It

When baseball season ended and school let out for the summer, the young teenager had a lot of time on his hands. Some days he would ride to work with his mom and hang out at the shopping center, but that got old quickly. On other days he would walk through the woods shaking dead pine trees until they fell or dig through trash piles along the road, looking for old and discarded bottles, or he'd roam the neighborhood with his new friend David. David and Tony became good friends. They spent the night with each other, rode bikes together, and occasionally would go through the nearby junkyard looking through wrecked cars for bottles and change.

During the weeks following her attempt to convince her son to move back to his dad's place, Tony noticed a lot of changes in his mom's behavior. Sometimes during the week, she would call and say she was going to be home late. She would tell Tony he could spend the night with David, or she would ask David's mom to let him spend the night with Tony. She would leave pizza money when the boys stayed at her house, and she would pay David's mom to feed Tony when he stayed with them. On some weekends she would drop Tony off at Betty or Barbara's house, and he didn't see his mom again until Sunday morning.

One night Tony was supposed to stay with David, but at the last minute, they had a family emergency, and Tony had to stay home. Since he didn't know where his mom was, he had no way of letting her know he was alone. Since Tony had been a latchkey kid since he was eleven, being alone wasn't an issue, so he just hunkered down for the long night with some snacks and his TV. He waited up for his mom as long as he could, but when the national anthem started playing on the TV, signaling the end of the broadcast day, he went to bed. Around 2:00 am, he woke up and looked in his mom's room, and she wasn't there. This frightened Tony, so he headed toward the kitchen to call the police. As he started to turn into the kitchen, he looked in the living room and seen his mom sitting beside a strange man who was lying on the floor.

Tony was in shock. He didn't know what to say, so he asked, "When did you get home?"

His mom sat up straighter and replied, "I've been home for about an hour."

Tony could tell something wasn't right. His mom's eyes were glassy, her speech was slurred, and she was acting strange.

"C'mere, I want you to meet my new boyfriend."

Tony stood in the hallway, raised his hand, and said, "Hi." Having seen drunk people before, Tony knew his mom had been drinking, so he turned to go back down the hall and said, "I'm going back to bed. I was just making sure you were home."

"I thought you were spending the night with David."

"They had a family emergency, so I had to come home, but it's okay, goodnight." Tony, feeling uncomfortable about the situation, hurried back down the hall to his room, shut the door, and locked it.

This wasn't the first time Tony had woken up and found a strange man in his house. It happened one Saturday morning when they lived in the boarding house in Cartersville. When Tony went to bed, he and his mom were the only people in the home. When Tony got up the next morning, there were three people in their home. His mom had snuck a man in after Tony went to bed. As she was getting ready for work, she kept telling the man over and over, "I have to go to work, and you need to leave. I'll call you when I get off this afternoon."

But instead of leaving, he kept insisting on staying until she got off.

"I don't have anything to do today, so I can stay here with . . .." The strange man looked at Tony and asked, "What's your name, son?"

The confused and nervous twelve-year-old looked at his mom, then looked at the strange man, and replied nervously, "Uh . . . Tony."

"Yeah, I'll stay here with Tony until you get off." The man walked up to his mom, pulled her up close by her hips, squeezed her real hard, and said, chuckling, "Then we can party some more!"

Feeling embarrassed at the man's behavior, she pulled away, telling Tony she would come home at lunchtime and check on him and, if he needed her before then, to call her at work. But the lunch counter at Woolworth's was busier than normal, and because someone called out, Tony's mom couldn't leave to come home for lunch. She did call Tony and check on him as promised, and she told the man that she would leave a little earlier since she didn't get a lunch break, but she didn't know what time that would be. But as the hours passed, he got bored with Tony and got angrier with his mom because she didn't come home when he expected her to.

"Why hasn't your mom come home yet?" The man asked as he paced around the small living area, directing his hostile questions at Tony. "She said she was coming home early. Why hasn't she called to let me know when?!"

Although Tony was happy having someone to play Crossfire and Rummy with earlier, he was getting scared now at the man's uncontrolled rage and anger. After calling Woolworths several times to reach her by phone failed, the man stormed out of the boarding house, cussing her and Tony as he left. Tony got up from the kitchen table where he had been observing the man's bizarre behavior, locked the door, and then sat back down in the same chair farthest from the door. He was thankful the man had left but was still feeling fear and anxiety. He had heard stories, stories of situations like his that didn't end well. He had never been that scared in his life, not even when his dad was angry. His mom was always close by, but today she was at work, and he was at home alone with a strange man with anger issues.

"Why did Mom put me in this situation?" His heart was racing. "How could she just leave me here alone with someone I don't know, and she hardly knows? He could've been a serial killer! Did he have a knife . . .

did he leave to go get a gun? Who knows what could have happened to me! What would I have done if he had attacked me? How could I have defended myself? Is he coming back?"

Many anxious and concerning thoughts rushed through the young-ster's mind as he slowly began to relax and let down his defenses. He began to question his mom's motives, her judgment, and even her love for him. He had never doubted her love before, but how could you put someone you love in this situation? Tony was still sitting in the same place an hour later, trying to make sense of it all, when he heard the key slide into the lock.

His mom opened the door and immediately asked, "Where's Johnny?"

"He got tired of waiting, so he left." Tony began to tell his mom what happened. "I need to tell you about Johnny . . ."

Noticing the Crossfire game and the deck of cards on the table, his mom quickly interrupted, "Did you two have fun playing games today?"

"Yes, we did for a little while, then he got bored and started . . ."

"Well never mind him . . ." interrupting again, "I'm going to go across the hall and take a shower if no one is using the bathroom right now. When I get dressed, we'll go out and get some supper. The counter was busy today, and I made a lot of tips," she said, smiling. "I think it's this new short uniform." She put her hands in the pockets of her short white outfit and jiggled the large cache of change. "Some of the coins are silver. I'll give you those for your coin collection."

"Thanks Mom, that's great!" Tony answered with excitement. He was always happy to get new coins for his coin books, and his mom's tips were a great resource for getting those old coins.

"I'll hurry. Just be ready to go when I get out."

"I'm already ready," Tony replied.

Tony's mom started emptying her pockets and putting her change on the table. "You can look through all this while I get ready."

Tony never told his mom about Johnny, his bizarre actions, and how he feared for his life. He also never told her about how it impacted his love and respect for her. He put those thoughts and feelings in the back of his mind as he searched through her change for wheat pennies, old nickels, and silver coins. But one year later, the thoughts and concerns are at the forefront of his mind again.

She's brought another strange man into our house while I was sleeping. It's not Johnny, but it could be someone like Johnny, or worse. She's picking these men up at bars and clubs and bringing them into our home! How could she endanger us like this? Tony was angry. *Is her lust worth endangering our lives? How many strange men has she brought in our home while I was sleeping or away for the night? How many more will she bring in before something bad happens to one, or both of us?"*

Tony was lying on his bed, listening and wondering, when he heard a vehicle start. He jumped up, went to the window, and peeked through the curtain to see if his mom was leaving him alone with another strange man again. Since the porch light was on, he could see that the only person in the car was the stranger. He watched as the shiny late model Cadillac pulled out of the driveway and headed down the street. Once the car was out of sight, Tony eased over to his bedroom door, unlocked it, and crawled back in bed. He could hear his mom scuffling down the hallway, sliding her hand along the paneling as she staggered to her bedroom and shut her door. Feeling anxious and uneasy about what had just happened, Tony laid on his back, staring up at the ceiling, thinking . . .

Doesn't she realize these men could be dangerous? Doesn't she realize she's being . . . Tony didn't want to say the word. It was a horrible word. But she had used it to describe loose women she worked with and others she knew, so he said it out loud, "A whore? How could she love me and do this? She doesn't care about anyone but herself. Maybe I should've agreed to go back to Dad's with her. She never brought strange men home when we lived there." Tony, thinking about what he had just said, laughed and whispered out loud, "Dad would've killed them . . . and her!" He chuckled again as he tried to make light of his situation. "Maybe I should let her know how I feel this time." Starting to feel sleepy, he rolled over on his side and said, "I'll talk to her . . . (yawn) . . . tomorrow."

Just like before, Tony never talked to his mom. He just learned to live with her new promiscuous lifestyle, avoiding her men friends when he could, and being polite and tolerant when he couldn't. Over the next few months, his mom became more wicked and more distant from Tony, often avoiding conversations with him and even sending him away for extended periods because she knew he didn't approve of her drinking and sleeping around, even though he never brought it up.

Because of her partying, she began to miss days at work and would often show up late because of a hangover or leave early to go clubbing. This started affecting her income since she wasn't working as many hours and didn't make as many tips.

Tony would come home after being gone for a week and find unopened certified letters on the table. When Tony answered the phone, it was usually a call from a collection agency. The Dodge Demon mysteriously disappeared. It was replaced by an older model Chevrolet that was purchased by one of her men friends. It smoked and got horrible gas mileage. People began knocking on the door looking for his mom. Clothes would go for weeks without being washed, either because his mom didn't have the money for the laundry mat or she was too busy partying.

Shortly after school started back, Tony got up one morning to get ready, and all he had clean was a pair of dress pants he hadn't worn in over a year that were tight around the waist and three inches too short, a dirty, wrinkled shirt out of the clothes hamper, and a pair of mismatched socks he found in his drawer. He was truly embarrassed to go to school dressed like that, but he had no other choice.

While sitting in history class, his teacher noticed his mismatched socks and asked him in front of the entire ninth grade class, "Tony, did you get dressed in the dark this morning?" Tony looked up from his test paper confused and asked, "What do you mean?" He had tried to keep his pants pulled down so no one would notice, but his pant legs had slid up when he sat down in the desk, exposing his socks. "You're socks, they're not the same color. One's blue, and one's black," she said, snickering. Tony wanted to climb under his desk and hide. The entire class began looking under their desk to see his socks. They also started snickering and poking fun at the embarrassed teenager, but to minimize the damage, he looked down at his socks and replied, "I guess I did."

He was so angry at his mom and his teacher for the embarrassment he endured. It was so devastating to him that he never forgot the incident. It was years before he forgave either of them, and he's not sure if he ever forgave them at all. He still gets mad when he thinks about the incident.

Tony knew his mom was struggling financially, but he didn't realize how bad things were until a cousin brought him home one Saturday afternoon at the end of a weeklong stay with relatives. His mom was at work, so he went into his playroom to watch some TV and wait on her to come home and fix supper. Since she didn't come home when she was supposed to, and since Tony hadn't eaten anything since breakfast, he was hungry, so he got up from his soft chair and started rummaging through the kitchen cabinets, looking for something to eat. But there was no food in the cabinets. No canned goods, no cereal, no bread, no saltine crackers, no peanut butter, no jelly . . . nothing. He looked through every cabinet, hoping to find something . . . anything . . . but there was no food to be found. He thought, *Surely there's something in the refrigerator*. He opened the refrigerator and, to his surprise, there was nothing in it but a jug of ice water and a few condiments. He closed the door, leaned back against the counter, and thought, *We're doomed*.

For the first time in Tony's life, he knew what it was like to be hungry. Not hungering after something you like and not being able to have it, but a different type of hunger, a hunger that comes from being hungry and not being able to satisfy the hunger with food.

"She has spent all our money on booze," the angry fourteen-year-old said as he slammed his fist down on the counter. "Her partying and drinking have cost us our new car . . . me being able to wear clean clothes . . . now food . . . and from the looks of things . . . the damn house!"

Tony's mom had told him she was looking for another place to live and that they may be moving to an apartment in south Atlanta, not far from her sister Barbara. He remembered her words from a few weeks earlier, "You can go to the same school with Marty, and since he's driving now ya'll can hang out, go fishing, and spend the night with each other like you used to."

It was now evident that the move she referred to wasn't because she wanted to be close to her sister or so he could spend time with his cousin, but she was losing the house to foreclosure.

"Ninety-eight dollars." Tony shook his head, then shouted, "Ninety-eight FRICKING DOLLARS A MONTH! How could she lose the house when the payment is less than twenty-five dollars a week?! She's made that in one day before . . . many times! This was supposed to be my 'forever' home!" Tony wanted to throw something, hit the wall, kick the door, run outside, and scream at the top of his lungs, but he didn't; he just walked slowly to his playroom, flopped down in his soft chair, and tried to calm down. He pushed his long black hair behind his ears and let out a long sigh as he reviewed the events of the past few months in his mind. He began to name aloud the things he felt were the root cause of his mom's downfall and the reason for their current situation. "Booze . . . lust . . . cigarettes . . . partying . . . whoring around . . . missing work with hangovers . . ."

Realizing his misery, hunger, confusion, pain, heartache, and dire situation was due to his dad's abuse, his mom and dad's neglect, the multiple schools, being pawned off on relatives, the divorce, her drinking, and other sins of his parents, Tony made a promise that day. "It doesn't matter what I have to do, how many jobs I have to work, or how much crap I have to put up with, I am going to be a good father, a dedicated husband, and I will NEVER allow my wife or especially my children to go through the hell I've had to endure all of my life! They're going to play baseball or other sports; they're going to have food to eat, nice clean clothes to wear, and they are going to have a dad in their lives who loves them, who will be there for them, and be in their lives continually!

To try and calm down, Tony took a deep breath, slowly let it out, and then looked around his playroom where he had spent many hours over the past fourteen months. He thought about how wonderful his life had been since he and his mom moved to Kennesaw.

"I'm going to miss this place," Tony said as his anger began turning to sorrow. "I've had some good times here . . . I just wish they could continue." As he looked at all the things he would have to box up for the move, his thoughts quickly changed to the apartments his mom had mentioned.

"Lord, I hope we're not moving into government housing again."

Two weeks later, the moving truck his mom was driving pulled into a parking space in front of their new apartment on Penfield Circle in south Atlanta just off Jonesboro Road, one mile north of I-285. Tony looked at the three white cinder block buildings with grey, black-stained shingle roofs that surrounded an overgrown, uncut grassy courtyard. Since Tony could still remember the last time he and his mom moved into an apartment, he was paying particular attention to the sidewalks. He had noticed on the way in that the sidewalk that started at the entrance of the complex ran along both sides of the street, separating the parking spaces from each courtyard. He also noticed that there was an adjoining sidewalk encasing the courtyard that gave access to each apartment building.

At least these sidewalks aren't broken to pieces, he thought.

The courtyard had an upward slope for about twenty yards and then leveled out for another 80 yards ending in front of the rear apartment building. The other two apartment buildings were across the courtyard from each other.

Tony looked up, down, and across the street and saw that most of the apartment buildings were identical and laid out in the same horseshoe pattern. He could see rusty clothesline poles at the rear of each building, but since he was fourteen now, he didn't look to see if there was a playground. He immediately knew he and his mom were moving back into government projects. For Tony, it was Deja vu. Remembering the last time they moved into government housing, he let out a long sigh and asked his mom, "Which apartment is ours?"

"We're in the building to the left, the first apartment closest to the street."

Trying to say something positive, Tony replied, "At least it's a one-level apartment. There are no stairs to climb."

Other than the occasional battery stolen out of their vehicle, a few missing hubcaps, someone breaking into their apartment in broad daylight and stealing Tony's shotgun his mom had given him for Christmas when he was twelve, the drug deals taking place in the apartment building across the courtyard, and the random gunshots heard off in the distance, living in the projects wasn't that bad.

Tony missed his school, his friends, and especially the house in Kennesaw. During the winter, the tiny apartment was much colder since there was square vinyl tile on the floor instead of carpet and an old gas furnace instead of an energy efficient electric system. It was much hotter during the summer since the central air conditioning had been replaced by an occasional wind blowing through one of the three-foot-by-one-foot rolled-out windows and a fan sitting on the floor in front of an opened door.

It was quite a change for the young teenager, going from the newly built three-bedroom home with the latest appliances to the old rundown apartment with a smelly pull handle refrigerator and a rusty old ceramic stove. But over time, he adapted to the changes and accepted his new surroundings. His mom continued her partying, drinking, and promiscuous ways, but since Tony stayed away from the apartment as much as he could, he hardly noticed. He spent a lot of time with his cousin Marty as his mom had suggested, and since Marty was sixteen now, had his own car, and was driving, the two went fishing, camping, swimming, watched movies at the Thunderbird drive-in theater, visited distant relatives, and rode around looking for girls.

A highlight of moving to Blair Village for Tony was getting to meet a chubby redheaded boy named Dennis Daviss. He lived in the apartment building at the rear of the courtyard and was the same age as Tony. They became close friends and stayed close until Tony lost contact with him after moving in with his Aunt Alice in the fall of 1975. Tony and Dennis reconnected years later when Dennis saw Tony doing a local TV show on a cable channel in Newnan.

Since Dennis was retired from the Georgia State Patrol, and Tony was self-employed, he and Tony were able to spend a good bit of time together. The two would meet with their wives and have dinner, and they went hunting together, talked on the phone regularly, and met for lunch at least once a month to talk about guns, politics, Walter F. George, the

Civil War (Dennis was a Civil War expert), and share their own war stories about living in Blair Village. They even attended their twenty-fifth
class reunion together.

Dennis and Tony were about as opposite as two friends could be,
with Tony being a preacher who never used profanity and Dennis being
unchurched most of his life who used profanity in simple everyday conversation. He wasn't vulgar; it was just who he was. He was a plain-
spoken person without a filter. Tony would get on him occasionally, but
it didn't do much good, although he was able to convince his friend to
visit the church he was pastoring in Fayetteville one Sunday.

Now everyone who knew Dennis knew he wasn't raised in or around
church, so he had never established any church etiquette. The Sunday
Dennis and Dana visited, the service went really well that morning. Many
people were moved by the Spirit of God and came to the altar, knelt, and
wept. Some stood at their pew and wept, including Dennis and Dana.
Tony could tell his friend was experiencing something he had never felt
before. It was amazing. After service was over, Tony was standing in
the vesta view, shaking hands and saying goodbye to the congregants
when Dennis came out of the sanctuary, still wiping tears. The large 400-
pound man walked up to Tony, gave him a hug, and said, "I enjoyed the
hell out of that." Shocked at what his friend just said but knowing how
Dennis was, Tony smiled and responded, "I'm glad you did my friend .
. . I'm glad you did!" The two stayed in touch until Dennis passed away
in October 2014.

Not to be a financial burden to his mom, who was making less money
now since being downsized to an assistant manager at the Woolworths
lunch counter inside Greenbrier Mall in East Point, Tony resumed collecting bottles and cashing them in at Thrift Town, the corner store near
the entrance of the apartments.

But the determined hard-working bottle collector didn't need to collect bottles long. His Aunt Barbara found out that the grocery store where
she shopped and where her sons Kenneth and Marty worked needed a
bag boy. Even though Tony was only fourteen, the manager hired him
at the request of his aunt, and within a few weeks of moving to Blair

Village, Tony was able to land his first real job in the grocery department at Treasure Island about a mile from his home. He started out making $2.10 an hour.

The managers, knowing Tony didn't have his own transportation, were able to schedule their new young employee close to the same hours as Marty. Tony and Marty rode to school together, rode to work together, and when they got off, Marty would drop Tony off at his apartment, which was directly on his route to his home on Blair Villa Drive. Tony couldn't have asked for a better first job. This worked out well, at least up until Marty decided to flip the assistant manager a bird. Marty tried to convince his assistant manager that it was a "Hawaiian Peace Sign," but he didn't buy it, so Marty got fired. But not having a ride to work didn't deter or discourage the determined bag boy. When his Aunt Barbara, Marty or one of his other relatives couldn't give him a ride to work, he would hitchhike. He knew it was more dangerous than when he hitchhiked in Kennesaw, but he felt like if he was ever going to leave the projects, he didn't have a choice, and the risk was well worth the reward. If he didn't get picked up, he just walked the entire distance. When he got off, his mom or Aunt Barbara would pick him up or one of his co-workers would take him home.

Not long after turning fifteen, Tony was trained to work in the pickup lane, an area outside the store where customers would drive around to pick up their groceries and the clerks would load them in their cars. Working the pickup lane was every bag boy and stocker's dream because that's where a clerk got paid a lot of extra money from tips, especially on Saturday and Sunday. Since Treasure Island, a division of the JC Penny Company, paid double time for working on Sunday, Tony began to see some nice paychecks.

Tony started making more money working part-time than his mom was making working forty hours a week. This was both a blessing . . . and a curse. It was a blessing in the sense that Tony was able to help his mom with groceries, utilities, gas, and other amenities, including a new set of tires for her car. He also started buying his own clothes, shoes, lunches, school supplies, and even a few luxuries, including a trolling motor (he didn't even own a boat) and some nice fishing gear. Just before his sixteenth birthday, he paid cash for his first car. It was a candy apple red, 1963 Ford Galaxie 500 that was sitting on blocks at his Aunt Betty's house. He purchased it from his uncle Buddy for seventy-five dollars. It was a curse in the sense that his mom told him he could start smoking when he could afford to buy his own cigarettes. Tony had been sneaking around smoking since he was twelve, but now that he was making good money, he was able to stop hiding his habit and smoke openly in front of his mom and other relatives without being reprimanded. It was also a curse since co-workers at Treasure Island had introduced him to marijuana at the young age of fifteen, and he used this new income source to buy the illegal substance to smoke himself and sell at school to others.

But Tony's pot smoking, drug dealing, and whoremongering came to a swift end just before his eighteenth birthday when he was charged with a felony and sentenced to one year in prison. If there's enough interest, that story may appear in another book in the not-too-distant future.

Tony's mom beside the Christmas tree in Kennesaw. She loved Douglas firs.

A man friend of Tony's mom named Loomus. Tony wanted his mom to marry him,
but she said he was too old.

Tony's mom and her friend Roberta getting ready to leave for a Halloween party.
Tony and Roberta's son Skip still talk occasionally.

Tony wearing an unwashed wrinkled shirt he took out of the dirty clothes hamper. He also needed a haircut.

Blair Village Apartment building.

The Drive-In theater on Jonesboro Road. And you thought The Fast and Furious was a new movie.

Tony's senior picture from Walter F. George High School. He was sixteen at the time this was taken.

CHAPTER XIV
Meet the Chow Hound

After several minutes of watching the parking lot with no one else pulling in, the funeral associate made his way down the hall to where everyone had gathered. "Is everyone here?"

Tony replied, "Everyone but my oldest daughter, but she'll be along soon."

"I'll go get Brian," the funeral associate responded.

"Brian is the funeral director who helped us make Marilyn's arrangements," Donnie announced to the group as the associate was leaving. "He's a really great guy."

"I couldn't have done this without him," Tony commented. "He was a great help when we were making the arrangements."

As the family continued talking, Brian approached, introduced himself, and shook hands with everyone.

"Are you the minister?" Brian asked as he shook Geoffrey Zimbelman's hand.

"I am," Geoffrey smiled. "How'd you know?"

"Other than Tony, you're the only other person wearing a coat," Brian said cheerfully.

Brian turned to Tony and Donnie and asked, "Are you ready?"

Tony sighed and replied, "Yes, sir."

Bryan stepped in front of the parlor doors, turned, and faced the family, and asked the minister to say a prayer.

The minister Geoffrey Zimbleman is known to most of the family as Brother Z. He's a longtime friend of Tony's who served as assistant pastor at the time Marilyn started coming to Bible Fellowship Church, a work Tony pioneered in 1996 in the studio of the radio station he owned at the time. He pastored the church until the station was sold in 2005.

Brother Z is a tall and slender gentleman in his mid-sixties. He still has a head full of dark brown hair, and his slim "Abraham Lincoln"-style beard enhances his long face and manly and athletic appearance. He is a very close friend of the family and is truly loved by everyone.

Marilyn thought a lot of Brother Z and is one of the reasons Tony asked him to help with the service. Marilyn would often comment to other church members how good-looking he was, but she'd always end her comments with, "He's way too young for me," or "Too bad he's married." Most people would laugh but in Tony's mind, he was thinking, "Even salvation doesn't change some things."

After Brother Z had finished praying, the director opened the white double doors and stepped aside. The entry room was a small gathering area with two high-back chairs with a light-colored pattern of various flowers, a matching love seat, and three accent tables. Each table had a plant or flower arrangement displayed, and there were a few plants and flowers on the floor along the wall. As the doors opened, you could immediately smell the distinct pleasant scent of fresh flowers. The scent was warming yet enlightening. It brought Tony back to a reality he was avoiding just moments earlier and the reason he was here. He paused before entering, thinking about death as the scent triggered memories of other funerals he had preached. Then he thought to himself, "Death is so cold, so final, so . . . painful."

As Tony and Donnie entered through the parlor doors, Tony caught a glimpse of Marilyn's lifeless body in the adjacent room, lying in the casket that he had just picked out twenty-four hours earlier. Tony was hesitant to go into the adjacent room, so he stalled by inspecting each plant and flower and looking at each card, although not really reading any of them. Donnie followed him around the room, staying close by his side.

After he looked at the last flower and card in the parlor, he glanced at the family, looked at his wife, and then looked at the casket, trying to unsee what he was seeing. He focused his attention on the large arrangement on top of the closed part of the casket that Brother Z had helped him purchase. He looked at the sprays that were standing to the left and the right of the coffin. Since the viewing room was adjacent to the chapel, he looked at the guests who had stepped just inside the large doorway while he was looking at flowers and reading cards.

So many emotions were surging through his body. His heart was racing, and he was breathing heavily. He did not know if he should cry, pray, or walk out! He had never experienced a grief like this. He had buried loved ones before, his Aunt Alice, his father-in-law, cousins, and he even played the piano at his dad's funeral, but this was different! The pain and anxiety were overwhelming! So much hurt and regret were buried deep inside him. Bad memories and unanswered questions surrounding him and Marilyn. It was so up setting that he was visibly shaking. With all the questions left unanswered and all the things left unsaid, why wouldn't he be; he's fixing to say his last goodbyes to . . .!

"Butch is on his way," Donnie interrupted Tony's thoughts as she squeezed her shaking husband's hand.

"Huh?" Tony turned to his wife, took a deep breath, relaxed a little, and said, "Thank the Lord. When did you find out?"

"I just got a text from him," Donnie continued. "He left the airport about an hour ago, so he should be here any minute."

Butch is Tony's first cousin and longtime hero. His real name is James Allen, but since he was born in an army hospital and had a huge appetite, one of the nurses started calling him "Butch the Chowhound." His family eventually dropped "the Chowhound" and just called him "Butch." He embraced his nickname proudly by sporting a military style flat-top most of his life.

He is twelve years older than Tony but only five years younger than his Aunt Marilyn. His mother Betty is one of Marilyn's older sisters, and since his family lived near his grandparents in Riverdale, the two became close. They went to the same school, rode the same bus, and even shared some of the same teachers.

Butch is six feet tall with a medium build and has been Tony's closest confidant his entire life. He was shot in the shoulder in Vietnam during combat, but he never let that experience change him from being the loving, caring, and tender person he is.

His dad Artis Allen preached many tent revival meetings during the late fifties and early sixties. He also pastored the same church on Highway 3 in Jonesboro, Georgia that Donnie's daddy, Bobby Gene Stapp later pastored. It's also the same church where Tony and Donnie met and were later married.

Artis was a prominent and respected man; a lot of people thought highly of the backwoods country preacher. Even though his wife supported his ministry, she wasn't a fan of the strict lifestyle she and their children had to live. When he tragically lost his life in a high-rise building fire in downtown Atlanta in 1968, it shocked the family and the communities he served. So many people turned out to pay their respects to the minister they loved; his funeral procession was over two miles long. Tony still remembers the long, slow ride behind the hearse to the cemetery as he sat in the rumble-style seat with his two cousins, Steve and Gerald, in the back of the late model Ford station wagon his Aunt Betty and Uncle Artis owned.

Artis performed a lot of weddings for family and friends and even officiated Tony's mom and dad's wedding. Butch has four younger brothers, but he is the only one to continue in his father's ministerial footsteps. He started preaching when he was sixteen and, shortly after being drafted into the army at eighteen, he preached an Easter service, and the other soldiers started calling him "Preach."

When Butch married his wife Glenda, they moved into the same townhome complex that Tony and his parents lived in. Even though Tony's parents didn't attend church, they allowed Tony to go to church on Sunday with Butch and Glenda. Tony would sit in Butch's Sunday school class with such anticipation and excitement. Butch was a great storyteller, which is why Tony loved being in his class. Instead of just reading and teaching the Bible, Butch would tell stories with a great deal of detail that made the stories come alive in his mind. Tony's favorite stories he learned while sitting in Butch's Sunday school class were "Jonah and the Whale" and the story of "Joseph."

Butch would often tell Tony, "You have a heart for God. God has a special purpose for you, so you just follow Him, and He's going to use you and do great things for you."

Tony hung on to these encouraging words and still cherishes them today. While he was being ignored at home and called nasty names, he would think of the encouraging words his cousin told him. After only a few months, Butch and Glenda bought a home in Fairburn, Georgia, and the newlyweds moved from Amulet Villa, and so did Tony's ride to church.

Even now, when Tony has a problem or a life issue, he calls Butch for prayer, counseling, and advice. And today is no different. Tony needs Butch; he needs answers, he needs his advice, and more importantly, he needs his spiritual support.

James Butch Allen. Taken in 2022.

Rev. Artis Allen, Marilyn & his son Butch. Photobombing started in the 1950's.

CHAPTER XV

GATHER AROUND THE CASKET

"It doesn't seem real," Tony whispered. "We were just with her on Saturday."

Donnie cradled her distraught husband's arm in hers, pulled herself close, and softly whispered, "It'll be okay."

Tony sighed as he tried to relax. Then the couple walked arm in arm slowly to Marilyn's casket. Brother Z walked up and stood beside Tony while everyone else watched in silence from a few feet away, giving Tony some time alone. Tony began to weep as he stroked Marilyn's long grey hair.

"Isn't she beautiful?" Tony said as tears rolled down his cheeks.

No one said a word. They knew Tony hadn't directed his question toward anyone.

Tony turned to Brother Z and said, "She's home!"

Then he turned to everyone else and said aloud, "She's home . . . she's home."

"She sure is!" Brother Z replied. "This is just where she used to live!"

At that point, Tony's cousin Sandra came up and stood by him, and they hugged each other and wept. Since Sandra didn't marry until she was in her forties, and since there were only eleven years in age difference between her and her Aunt Marilyn, they shared a lot of common interests, including great food, shopping, and the Atlanta Braves.

After Marilyn's sister Barbara died, which is also Sandra's mother, she began to spend more time with Marilyn and made it her mission to see that her aunt had everything she needed. Marilyn lived in an apartment in

Christian City Retirement Center in Union City, Georgia, for years and was only twenty minutes from Sandra and her husband.

When Marilyn started showing signs of dementia, and the family took away her car, Marilyn became furious. Being that Marilyn was a very stubborn and independent individual, she did not like people telling her what to do or doing things for her. But knowing she was not in any condition to drive, Sandra took it upon herself to take her aunt to the store, the doctor, out to dinner, or anywhere Marilyn wanted to go, with the exception of the beach. Marilyn did tell Sandra she wanted to go to the beach before she died, but Sandra was not sure if it was the dementia talking or the medicine.

After having a good cry with Sandra, Tony stepped to the side and sat down on a stool near the head of the casket to let others come close and pay their respects. He talked and laughed with everyone who was willing to share a memorable story with him.

Rachel stepped inside the parlor doors and walked up to her mom who was talking to Terry and Beverly Waldrop, longtime friends of Tony and Donnie's, and announced, "I finally made it."

"It's about time," Donnie said as she hugged her rain-soaked daughter. "I was beginning to get worried."

"All this rain . . . and TRAFFIC!" Rachel exclaimed with emphasis on traffic. "I think it's gotten worse since I moved to North Carolina."

"That's one of the reasons we moved to North Georgia!" Donnie said agreeably.

When they stopped hugging, Rachel stood for a moment, wiping rain droplets off her coat, then proceeded to hug the rest of her family, shake hands with friends she hadn't seen in a long time, and introduced herself to those she didn't know, making sure she greeted everyone in the parlor and chapel. Tony smiled, admiring his daughter making everyone feel welcome. As she made her way toward her dad, Tony stood up. As they embraced, Tony kissed her on the cheek and said proudly, "Still my social butterfly, I see . . . it's great to see you!"

"It's great to see you too, Dad. Are you okay?"

"I'm better . . . now that you're here." As they separated, Tony took his daughter's hand, and they stepped up to the edge of the casket. "Isn't she beautiful? Me and your mom picked out everything."

"She looks lovely, Dad, so beautiful."

Rachel noticed her dad had begun to cry softly. "You know she's in a better place now; no more suffering from Alzheimer's, no more not knowing who we are . . ."

"Yeah, I know, but I'm still going to miss her. I'm glad you had the opportunity to come home in July and see her. Those pictures we made with you and your kids are priceless."

Rachel began to show some emotion as she responded, "Me too, Dad . . . me too."

"She really loved and spoiled you, didn't she?"

"I was her favorite . . . that's for sure"

As Tony looked at his teary-eyed daughter, he suggested, "Go check out her memorial video in the chapel; it turned out really good."

Rachel wiped her eyes and said, "I need to get with Leah on what songs we're singing. Do you have any picked out that you want us to sing?"

"I'm leaving all of that up to you two, although I did hear a rumor that your brother may sing one."

"Caleb or Sam?" Rachel asked surprisingly.

Tony laughed. "Sam, of course."

"I was about to fall over if Caleb was singing tomorrow. He's never sang in public before."

"Well, I'm sure it would be a welcome blessing. If he wants to sing a solo, he can."

"He might sing 'so low' no one can hear him," Rachel said jokingly as she turned and then headed into the chapel. As she took her seat beside her siblings, Tony sat back down and began admiring all the things he had chosen for Marilyn's final moments. The dark grey casket with shiny chrome handles, the flowing purple skirt with matching jacket, the pink blouse, and the grey sheer scarf with different colored flowers draped beautifully around her neck—all these things made Marilyn look so beautiful and peaceful. But Tony didn't just pick these items at random; he had some help.

When he was moving Marilyn out of her apartment and into the house with him and Donnie, he found a notebook that contained a list of things she wanted carried out when she died, and Tony was determined to fulfill everything on her list. *The rest will be fulfilled tomorrow*, he thought as he noticed some new arrivals sitting in the chapel, watching the video presentation the funeral home had produced from the pictures he had provided them the day before.

Suddenly, Tony realized he was alone; no one was in the parlor with him. Everyone had followed Rachel into the chapel. He didn't like being alone, so he went into the chapel to greet his Aunt Carol and the other new arrivals and invite them into the viewing room to see Marilyn. As he greeted his Aunt Carol, who is the only sibling of Marilyn's still alive, he thought, *Surely, she has some secrets she needs to share with me.*

After Tony had welcomed everyone, he stepped back into the parlor to take a closer look at the plants and flower arrangements he had skimmed over when he first arrived. He noticed some were from elderly relatives who lived out of state, some were from his children and close family, one was from Keith and Brenda Brookshire, longtime friends of Tony and Donnie from Cartersville, and one from a company that Tony had done a lot of business with over the years. He smiled as he read every card. He was truly thankful for everyone who cared enough about him and Marilyn to send flowers or a plant.

Suddenly, as if you had turned a light on in a dark room, a burst of energy came walking through the parlor doors.

"Hey, cuz!" The deep but familiar soft tone the family knew all too well echoed through the parlor and chapel. "I made it!"

Tony turned to see a family figure he had not seen in years. Without hesitation, he grabbed his broad-shouldered cousin and gave him a big bear hug. "It's great to see you, Butch. It's great to see you!"

"Easy, easy!" Butch said laughingly as Tony was holding him tight. "My old bones aren't as strong as they used to be."

Tony laughed as he released his grip, then stepped back, admiring his tall grey-haired cousin, who is no longer sporting a flat-top. "Glad you could make it, Butch. It's so great to see you."

"Me too, cuz. Me too! Now where's 'em youngin's and grand youngin's you been telling me about?"

Before Tony could answer, Donnie, who had recognized the familiar voice, emerged from the chapel with an entourage of family members in tow.

Tony proudly pointed and said, "There they are!"

"Buuuuutch!" Donnie said, holding her arms out as she walked toward the preacher who she has an enormous amount of love and respect for. She went straight to him and gave him a big hug as she gently whispered, "I'm glad you came. Tony really needs you right now." Butch whispering back, replied, "I know, but I believe he'll be fine once I explain everything."

"I hope so; he's a mess," Donnie said as she stepped back to give access to others who were waiting to greet the charismatic gentleman.

Butch recognized Tony's children immediately since their dad kept his picture-collecting cousin up to date with current photos. He complimented them on how great they looked and how much they had changed since he had last seen them. Sam proudly introduced his wife and children, then Rachel showed Butch current pictures of her children as she explained why she left them with their dad in North Carolina.

"Aunt Carol, you look great!" Butch spoke softly as his last living aunt approached and gave him a gentle hug.

"Thank you! I feel great too. You know I'm eighty-one now," Carol responded proudly.

"Yes ma'am, and you don't look a day over fifty!"

Aunt Carol welcomed her nephew's compliment with a huge smile. She always announces her age after she greets someone, something she would have never done forty years ago.

Tony heard his aunt talking about her age and began to wonder, *At what age do women stop hiding their age and start bragging about how old they are?* He chuckled to himself as he watched her turn and head back into the chapel.

The rest of the family greeted the Atlanta native who now calls South Louisiana home with compliments, handshakes, and a lot of hugs. This went on for what seemed like an hour to Tony but was only for a few minutes. Rachel announced that she and Leah had to practice a few songs, so they headed back toward the chapel with their brothers following close behind.

Some family and friends followed the children back into the chapel and took a seat in one of the padded pews, waiting to hear the girls sing and curious to see if Sam or Caleb would bless them with a song. Many of the visitors said their goodbyes as Tony and Donnie thanked them for coming.

After everyone had exited the parlor, Donnie looked at Butch and said, "I'm going to go listen to the kids practice. I'll leave you two alone for a while. I know you guys have a lot of catching up to do." Butch nodded and winked as if to say, "I got this." Donnie smiled and nodded back as she turned and headed for the chapel. The soft sound of a piano was playing in the background as the two cousins sat down on the floral printed love seat in the now empty parlor. The answers Tony is searching for are about to be revealed, but before this night is over, he may be wishing he had left them hidden in the vast abyss of secrets.

CHAPTER XVI

LOVE, LIES, & FOREIGNER

Tony nervously touched his Apple watch, looked at the digital display, and said, "7:15. It seems later than that."

Butch asked, "What time is visiting hours over?"

"Not till 9:00."

Tony, knowing why Butch was there and trying to avoid diving into the secrets he knew were about to be revealed, asked him about his wife Glenda, his son Jeff, and his flight. Butch, after catching his cousin up on his family and his flight, finally asked, "You do know why I'm here, don't you?"

Tony sighed, then looked down at the floor, and replied, "Yeah . . . yes, I do."

"Donnie said you wanted some answers." The tone was changing from lighthearted to serious.

"I do, but I'm not sure if I'm ready to hear them. I have my suspicions, and there's been innuendos and whispers throughout my life, but I need to hear the whole truth from someone who knows the facts."

"You've known me a long time, Tony. Have I ever led you wrong?"

"No sir. You've always been straightforward with me, even when it hurt, and I'm sure this conversation will be no different."

Butch smiled with agreement and compassion as he wrestled for a way to start the conversation without seeming too anxious or being too hurtful. After finding the right words, he asked, "What did your mom tell you happened to your real father?"

"She told me," Tony paused, "she told me he was killed in a car wreck hurrying home to see me the day she brought me home from the hospital."

"But you do know that story is false, right?"

Tony took a deep breath, shook his head, and said, "Imagine living with the guilt, believing you were partly responsible for your real father's death. I began to believe that if I hadn't been born, he would still be alive. As I got older, whenever I questioned Mom about him, she would say, 'I don't want to talk about him right now,' or 'Can we discuss this some other time?' She never would give me a straight answer. When I was eleven, I asked if she had any pictures of him; she told me she burned them all. That's when I became suspicious. Even I knew then no one burns all the pictures of a deceased loved one, so to answer your question, yes, I do know the story is a lie."

"How did that make you feel, knowing your mother lied to you all those years?"

Tony leaned forward, looked up at Marilyn's casket, and said, "It wasn't easy, but I'm sure that's not the only lie she told me or the only secret she kept from me. Most of my life, Butch, I have felt like a castaway, a vagabond, a derelict floating aimlessly on the sea of life. I felt alone and betrayed by those who said they loved me, and though I put a smile on my face and looked happy, I was hurting inside. Now, I do not doubt their love. I just believe, in everyone's eyes, I was a mistake, an unimportant part of my mom's life, Vic's life, and, at times, even in the eyes of God. It's been hard dealing with everything."

"Things didn't seem that bad between you and your mom when we lived next door to you. What changed?"

"Now don't get me wrong, cuz," Tony continued. "I didn't feel the disconnect with Mom the first eleven years of my life. I felt like she loved me, and, at times, she would express her love for me, but not long after the divorce, she turned into a different person. She became a self-absorbed, independent, hateful narcissist. She didn't care about anyone but herself, her new lifestyle of drinking and partying, and her men. I became an 'inconvenience' and a 'burden' to her, and that's when we started drifting apart. It was as if . . ." Tony's voice began to crack as tears began to flow down his cheeks. "She was pushing me away and trying to get someone to take me off her hands. I didn't feel like she cared for me anymore, and I can honestly say it made me not care for her either, and . . . I hate that now!"

Tony wiped his eyes, then slapped his hands on his legs in frustration and said with a bit of anger, "Do you know how hard it was for me to pick out a Mother's Day card?! It was hard, I tell you; it was hard!"

Butch, seeing the hurt on Tony's face, interjected quickly, "It's okay. Calm down. I know you're feeling passionate right now."

Tony took a deep breath and said. "Sorry . . . it's just that . . . most of the cards would have sayings like 'Thanks, Mom, for being there for me,' or 'You've always been the person I could count on growing up,' and when I would read those cards, I would get angry because I didn't have a mother like that most of my life. In many ways, she was the opposite. I never found one that said, 'You were never there for me, but I love you anyway'!"

Tony stopped, looked at his concerned cousin, then looked at the casket and said, "Can you see now why I feel this way? The only solace I had was Donnie and the kids, and when that went south a few years ago and it almost . . ." Tony stopped and took a deep breath as he remembered the pistol he had retrieved from the nightstand, then continued. "Killed me."

"How are things with Sam and Leah now?"

"Better, but not where they used to be, and I am not sure if they ever will be. I believe I will die having failed as a father in the eyes of at least two of my children, maybe all of them, who knows, which, for decades, was my only real success I felt I had in life, and now even that's in question." Tony stopped for a moment as he was suppressing his emotions. Butch sat silent, letting his cousin share his true feelings, something he was sure he didn't do often. "I'm just a screw up, Butch, a real screw up. Why was I even born?" Tony began to weep quietly.

Butch sat watching as his cousin wept and wiped his eyes with the sleeve of his jacket. He reached and grabbed a few tissues from a box on the table beside him and handed them to Tony as he digested the words his brokenhearted cousin had just shared with him. After a moment, Butch put his hand on his shoulder and softly said, "Everyone makes mistakes, cuz . . . everyone"

"Well then, tell that to Leah!" Tony snapped back with a quiver in his voice. Then realizing he was out of character, said, "I'm sorry."

"It's okay. I know you have a lot of emotions going through that heart of yours right now."

Tony sat silent for a moment, then leaned back against the love seat and said tearfully, "Leah . . . was my anchor, Butch. When me and Donnie married, I truly believed it was the Lord's will, but I don't believe we loved each other back then like we do now. She was sheltered and spoiled all her life, she had parents who loved her dearly, and she grew up in a stable Christian home. I, on the other hand, grew up frightened most of my childhood, was constantly cussed at and called vulgar names, tossed around from place to place like a family heirloom no one wanted, and sometimes not knowing where my next meal was coming from. We were about as opposite as a couple could be, but we made it work even though we argued a lot the first couple of years. Most of our arguments were about money, but what made our relationship worse," Tony shook his head and smiled, "is that many of our arguments were over where we were going to church, Brother Crawford's or her dad's, and, as you know, this went on for quite some time."

Butch, seizing the opportunity to lighten the mood, interjected quickly, "You should have had that put in the wedding vows!"

"Well, you performed the ceremony; you should've put it in there." The two cousins laughed as they relaxed a little.

"I remember that," Butch continued, "You two had a hard time settling on a church."

"I was our church's piano player, and she was her dad's piano player, so that put us both in a 'spiritual tug of war' between the churches. It really created a lot of friction between us."

"Well, at least ya'll survived and can laugh about it now."

"Yeah, but it wasn't funny then. I tell people today that we have been '*happily married*' for thirty-eight years . . . and thirty-eight out of forty ain't bad!"

Butch grinned as he replied, "I'm sure Donnie agrees with that statement."

"She does, even though she doesn't like me to joke about it."

"I'm sure it doesn't stop you, though, does it?"

"Not at all!" Tony replied quickly. "I also tell people that we have never had an argument."

"Oh, really?" Butch asked curiously.

"It's true. We call them 'intense moments of fellowship' now!"

"You're a mess!" Butch laughed as he shook his head, then responded, "There's that joke-cracking cousin I'm used to."

Tony smiled, then looked over at Marilyn's body lying in the coffin. Realizing he had gotten off subject, he wiped the smile off his face and then continued. "As I was saying, cuz, when Rachel was born, I can't really explain that feeling; becoming a dad profoundly changed my life! I felt like a new person. I felt like . . . my life finally had purpose, meaning, and direction, and I had someone close to me who I could absolutely love and who would love me back, something I don't think I had ever experienced up to that point in my life. But as Rachel got older, she didn't really show love or affection very much, toward me or her mom. She was a very stubborn and independent child and didn't express her feelings often. But . . ." Tony paused as he wrestled with his emotions, then took a deep breath and continued, "when Leah came along, she was . . . I don't know how to explain it . . . she was . . . different. She had a heart of pure gold. When she was just learning to walk and talk, that girl would crawl in my lap, put her arms around my neck, squeeze, and say, 'I wuv you, Ditty.' That touched me so much. When I came home from work, she would usually be the first to greet me at the door, reaching out for me to pick her up so she could hug me. Many times, while I was holding her, she'd wrap her arms around my neck, lay her head on my shoulder, and hold on to me. If I tried to put her down, she would fight to stay in my arms. I had never experienced anything like it in my life. Now, don't get me wrong.

Rachel would be there too, but she would usually ask if I had candy or something to give her, but Leah was more interested in giving Daddy a hug than what I had in my pockets." Tony leaned forward and looked to his left at his cousin as they both listened to the music coming from the chapel, "Butch," Tony paused. "Leah saved me! I mean . . . really saved me. I felt like for the first time, I had somebody in my life who would love me unconditionally. It didn't matter that I had been to prison, what I did as a sinner, how bad my past was, or if I had money or a pocketful of candy or not, she just . . . loved me".

"Tony," Butch said concerningly, "you know Jesus is the only. . ."

Tony interrupted, "I know Jesus saved me spiritually, Butch, but Leah saved me . . . emotionally. Her tender heart and willingness to show me true love and affection began to heal the deep, embedded wounds and scars from my childhood. It was . . . magical . . . supernatural. She had a huge impact on me. It's just hard to explain."

Tony smiled as he thought of a memory, then continued. "During that time, I was sitting in a restaurant eating lunch when I heard a song come over their sound system. It was so smooth and gentle that I started listening to the lyrics. I later learned it was a song by Foreigner. The song brought back memories from my childhood, the loneliness, abuse, the rejection, and the feeling of being unloved. The song also reminded me that I had finally found the love I had been wanting and needing. When I heard, 'In my life, there's been heartache and pain,' and then 'Can't stop now, I've traveled so far to change this lonely life,' Butch, it got my attention."

Tony paused. He was trying to hold the tears back. He looked over at the casket, looked back at his cousin, and proceeded. "As I listened to the chorus, 'I want to know what love is, I want you to show me, I want to feel what love is, I know you can show me,' I felt like that song was letting me know my search for love was over, and I had finally found what being loved was all about, and a great part of 'knowing what love is' . . . well . . . was because of Leah. Her affection toward me was what I had searched for all my life, and I finally found it when she came along.

That's what I mean by 'she saved me.' She was a godsend, Butch . . . a true godsend."

Butch sat silent, looking, and listening.

Tony continued. "As she grew older, I leaned on her love even more, maybe even taking it for granted. Rachel got most of the attention because of her outgoing personality, but Leah was that silent rock who kept me strong, motivated, and focused. I believe God gave her to me to heal me, and as long as she was in my life, I didn't feel the pain and scars from my childhood, but now that she is drawn away and won't call, text, or have anything to do with me . . . well . . . it hurts. It's like being rejected by my mother all over again, and it's taken a heavy toll on me spiritually and emotionally. I guess that's why I'm so angry at her and why I lashed out at her when she ignored me. It's . . . painful."

"Have you told her any of this?"

"No, I haven't. She hasn't given me the chance. I've invited her to meet me for lunch or dinner on several occasions, but she declines every time. When we are around each other, it's like we're . . . strangers. She doesn't come around us unless other family members are present, and she hasn't visited us since we moved to Adairsville four years ago. She never calls; she might send a text occasionally, but it's usually after we've texted her, it's . . .." Tony paused, "what happened between me and my mom all over again except this is harder. Mom and I weren't that close, but Leah and I were very close. Plus, I fed her, clothed her, gave her a nice roof over her head, paid for her education, voice lessons, gave her on-the-job training, and even helped her land her first job, and this is the thanks I get! I don't know how to handle it! If she had been our only child, I would be in a mental institution by now."

"That doesn't sound like the Leah I remember," Butch responded.

"It's not the Leah I raised either! Thankfully, I still have Rachel, Sam, and Caleb who still include me in their lives." Tony smiled and then proceeded, "Hopefully out of those three, one of them will pick a nice nursing home for me!"

Butch laughed as he responded, "A benefit of having more than one child for sure."

"And this behavior started several years ago. I wrote a song to sing to her at her wedding called, 'Diddy,' in honor of the relationship we had since she was a child. I worked hard on that song, making sure it was specifically written for her. After the wedding, she complained that it wasn't as good as the songs that I had written about Rachel and Sam. I was shocked! I didn't know I was in a contest! She called me Diddy since she was old enough to talk, and I thought she would love it. Having her reject it so coldly hurt me. Shortly after that, she sent me a song to listen to called, 'You Can Let Go Now Daddy.' I took it that she was saying, 'Stop holding on to me.' I was hoping that wasn't the message she was sending, but it was. About a year later, her mom and I were having a meeting with her and Sam, and she plainly told both of us during that meeting that we needed to move on with our lives and not concern ourselves with them anymore. Add that to the song she sent me . . . the lack of interaction and . . . well, you can see why I feel the way I do." Tony thought for a minute, then asked his longtime mentor, "Do you have any suggestions?"

Butch, raising his eyebrows, replied, "Wow, that's surprising. Normally I would say to give it time, but it sounds like you've given it a lot of time already."

"I've been dealing with this for more than five years, and hardly a day goes by that I don't think about her and what I possibly could've done to cause her to be this way toward me and her mom. Whatever it is, or was, she's never told us."

"It may not be anything you've done. Think about it, you didn't do anything to your mom to cause her to reject you."

"That's true."

"Your mom turned into the person she did because of the choices she made and not because of what you did to her."

"I never looked at it that way."

Butch asked carefully, "Do you think it had anything to do with her . . . being . . ."

"I thought of that many times, wondering if she blamed me for what happened to her and Rachel. Of course, I had no idea it was going on, or

I would've stopped it. I don't see how they could blame me since when-ever we would ask them if anyone had ever touched them inappropriately, they would always say, 'No.' They were simply scared to tell us, I guess. Not learning about it until they were in their twenties just furthered my frustration. I was supposed to protect them and . . . I failed . . . so if she does, I deserve it." Tony sighed, then added, "Just add that to my list of screw-ups as a father."

Well, cuz," Butch responded confidently. "Despite the way Leah or anyone else feels about you, let me assure you, you're not a screwup or a mistake! I'm going to set the record straight here and now. You deserve to know the truth, and I'm going to give it to you straight!"

"That would be great, Butch, really great."

"You may not like what I'm going to tell you, and it might sting a little, but at least you'll have the answers you're searching for and obvi-ously need."

Tony's rock, sweet Leah. Children don't come any better than this child. And yes, she used to be told she looked like Laura Ingles from Little House on the Prairie.

Marty, Butch and Tony waiting in the church office just before Tony & Donnie were to be married. Butch officiated and Marty was the best man.

Tony and Donnie in their apartment shortly after being married.

CHAPTER XVII

DEAR GOD, WHAT DO I DO?

It was an unseasonably warm day for April in South Atlanta, Georgia. Butch and his younger brothers were taking advantage of the extremely nice weather playing outside in the front yard of their flat roof house on Waters Road. The 2000-square foot home was what Artis and Betty Allen needed for their large family of rowdy boys. On the left side of the house was a large screened-in porch that was twenty feet long and twelve feet deep and covered more than half of the front of the house, including the front door. It was large and shady enough to entertain family and friends when they would visit, and the never-locked screen door made it warm and inviting whenever family or friends would drop by. The large holes in the screens made it more fun for Butch and his brothers to jump through from all sides of the yard, but the tattered screens didn't do much to keep the mosquitos and other insects at bay.

Butch happened to be walking by the front porch when he noticed his Aunt Marilyn kneeling on the pine wood floor with her head in her hands, weeping. He looked and saw his mom standing in the doorway of the house, wiping tears from her face with her Apron. Concerned for his aunt and mom, the curious eleven-year-old slipped through one of the large holes in the screen and stood on the porch to see why they were crying. Before he could ask any questions, he saw his Grandad's truck pulling up in the yard. His Granny and Granddaddy exited their truck, talking and smiling about their adventures from their milk route that day. They had stopped by to check on their youngest daughter

Marilyn since they had not seen or heard much from her since she came to live with her oldest sister and her family a few months ago.

Marilyn had moved in with the Allens so she would be closer to her new job at the diner near Cleveland Avenue. John and Mattie Cox were just poor dirt farmers who lived around Clayton and Fayette County, Georgia, most of their lives. They had eleven children, although two died as infants shortly after birth. John and Mattie and their nine children, four boys and five girls, shared a small shotgun house most of their lives, although they did live in larger homes from time to time since John was a sharecropper and moved every few years.

The children worked hard growing, up milking cows, chopping wood, stringing barbwire, mending fences, fetching water from a creek or well, gathering eggs, making clothes, tending to cattle and horses, and harvesting fruits and vegetables. They even had to pick cotton by hand, which all the children swore they would never do again once they left home. They truly lived off the land.

One of the primary sources of income for the large family was the milk and egg route. John would load his truck up most mornings with fresh milk and eggs as well as seasonal vegetables and deliver these items to customers who were along his route. He and the family worked hard every week but did honor the Sabbath day, being that they were devout Southern Baptists. Their son-in-law Artis Allen tried to convince them to convert to holiness, but since John loved his pipe, and Mattie Mae loved her snuff, they decided to stay Southern Baptist.

As the old jolly couple walked up the rickety wooden steps, their demeanor changed when they noticed Marilyn on her knees in a fetal position in front of her sister Betty, crying uncontrollably. They could also tell that Betty had been crying as well.

As they walked onto the porch, Mattie stopped, looked up at her husband, then looked at her daughters and asked in a concerned yet assertive way, "What's the matter?"

Marilyn's crying became more intense.

Mattie, who was a petite woman, whose once thin figure had become proportionally round after eleven pregnancies, looked at her daughter

Betty and said with a louder stern voice, "Tell me what's the matter with Marilyn?!"

John, being a man of few words, stood silent, surveying the situation from a father's perspective and instinct. His tanned and weathered face was grimacing as he placed one hand in the pocket of his faded bib overalls, then with his other hand, he placed his neatly curved store-bought pipe between his teeth and took a puff, hoping that what his daughter was about to tell them was not what he was thinking.

"Ask Marilyn," Betty responded with a quivering voice.

Mattie knelt beside her shaking sixteen-year-old daughter, brushed her hair back, and asked softly, "What's the matter, honey?"

Marilyn looked up at her mom with tear-stained eyes and answered, "I'm . . . I'm . . . pregnant."

It took a lot of courage for the baby daughter of Mattie and John Cox to push those words out of her mouth. Saying those words in a conservative Southern Baptist home in the Deep South in 1958 was not easy to do.

"You're what?!" You could hear the shock and concern in Mattie's voice as she stood straight up.

Marilyn put her head back down and said a bit louder, "I'm pregnant!"

This was not what Mattie was expecting to hear from the lips of her baby girl.

"Dear God, Marilyn, how could you let this happen! We will have to move; we will be thrown out of the church! Your reputation is soiled!"

Mattie walked briskly back and forth across the long screened-in porch; her hard heels knocking like a hammer on each board as she put each foot down harder than she normally did when she walked. You could tell she was upset. She was sharing her opposition to the information she was trying to digest as her cotton dress twisted back and forth like a rope tree swing when she turned quickly as she encountered the end of the porch. Then she stopped and let out a scream, "Ahh!" and then walked off the porch to the truck. It was evident by her behavior that she had taken this news very hard.

Butch stood silent, looking at his favorite aunt, who was still kneeling on the porch over a puddle of tears. He was not familiar with the term "pregnant"; he had never heard that word before. He had heard adults say, "In the family way" before, but this new word was foreign to him. *Could she mean in the family way?* he thought. He had younger brothers, so he knew if that is what being pregnant meant, then there would be a baby here soon. *How is this possible?* the confused eleven-year-old reflected as he studied the situation. *Aunt Marilyn doesn't even have a husband.*

After her mom got in the truck and slammed the door, her dad pulled his pipe from his lips and asked calmly, "Whose is it?"

His lovely and attractive baby girl respected her father and would never lie to him, so she did not answer his question directly, but she did stop crying long enough to say, "A guy I met at the diner." Marilyn had recently taken a part-time position at a local diner in East Point and was working there for tips after school.

Knowing his daughter dodged his question, he asked, "What's his name?"

As Butch listened, he could tell his Aunt Marilyn was not giving up any information about the identity of the soon-to-be father. She told her dad that she knew what her brothers were capable of, and she did not want either of them going to jail for her mistake. John respected his daughter's position; he, too, knew what his boys were capable of. He lifted her up off the porch as she dusted the dirt off the knees of her rolled-up blue jeans, then pulled his frightened daughter up close to him, wrapped his arms around her, and said, "It'll be ok. Besides, with your brothers and sisters married and gone, and you working all the time, it will be rather nice to have another mouth to feed. Me and your mom are starting to have a lot of leftovers."

Marilyn put her arms around her consoling father, laid her head on his shoulder, and said, "Thanks Dad. I love you."

"I love you too, and so does your mom. She'll be ok. Just give her some time."

"Are you mad at me?"

Her dad thought for a moment before answering. "Not mad. Disappointed that you let this happen to you at such a young age, but not mad. You do know you will have to quit school after this year and work harder than you have ever worked in your life, don't you? Picking cotton will seem easy once you start providing for a baby; it's hard enough with two parents."

"I know, Dad . . . I'm really scared."

"You'll be seventeen in a few days, and you have several months to work and save before the baby gets here." John pushed his daughter away from him and held her at arms-length, making sure the pipe he was holding stayed away from her white cotton blouse. "Are you sure you can handle this? There are other options, you know."

Marilyn looked at her dad in shock. The thought of terminating the pregnancy before her parents found out had crossed her mind, but she immediately dismissed them, believing such an act would be murder to the baby and life-threatening to her. She had heard stories.

"Dad, you're not talking about . . . a . . . a . . ."

Her dad, knowing where she was headed, stopped her abruptly, "NO, honey, not that! I was thinking about adoption. As Christians, we could never allow such a gruesome task to take place in our family. That would be murder at the highest level. We'd both be headed to hell without mercy!"

Butch was still listening to the conversation from where he had been standing the entire time but did not understand a word his aunt or grandfather was saying other than hell because his dad had preached on it many times. His mother was still standing in the doorway, watching and listening to the conversation, and sighed and relaxed after her dad clarified his previous statement.

Marilyn, also relieved at her dad's answer, relaxed, and said, "I don't think I want to do that." She touched her tummy and said, "I want to raise this baby myself."

"The other option I was thinking about is a shotgun wedding," John began to further clarify his previous comment with a louder tone than before. "Any chance this fornicating whoremonger would be man enough to do the proper thing?" You could now hear a disdain for the mystery man in his disgruntled voice.

"I'm not sure, Dad. I haven't told him yet."

"You need to find out as soon as possible. The most logical thing to do at this point would be for you two to be married." John sighed, then continued, "And as you pointed out already, I'd hate to think what Jack or one of your other brothers will do to this man if he refuses."

As John started toward the screen door, Betty broke her silence and said, "Thanks for stopping by, Dad. Did you need anything?"

John turned, looked at his baby daughter, then back at Betty, and replied, "It can wait. Just tell Artis I stopped by." Then he walked off the porch and headed to his truck.

Word spread fast about Marilyn being "in the family way," and the word "rape" was being thrown around quite a bit among the older siblings since Marilyn was a virgin and only sixteen when she became pregnant. When Marilyn heard the threats that her brothers were making, she told the father of her child that he needed to marry her, or there was going to be trouble. After leading her on like they were going to get married for a few weeks, the father finally admitted that he was already married, and there was no way he was going to leave his wife and marry her.

Finding out that her pretending fiancé had lied to her about being married and had led her on about marrying her devastated the six-teen-year-old. When she told her family that he told her he was already married, they were infuriated and demanded that she tell them his name. But Marilyn was determined to keep his identity a secret for fear of someone seriously hurting him. But when Jack found out he was mar-ried and nearly ten years her senior, he went to the diner where his sister worked and shook down the employees and customers like a profes-sional sleuth until he had his name and where he worked.

Jack found out he was a suit salesman at a clothing store close to the diner. Just as Marilyn feared, Jack went to the store where the father of her child worked and confronted him. During the loud and angry exchange, Jack threatened to have him locked up for statutory rape if he didn't divorce his wife and marry his sister. He also threatened to have him fired and to tell his wife about his infidelity. The man insisted that Marilyn had told him she was over eighteen and that the sex was consensual, although Jack never believed him or Marilyn's account of the situation.

Fortunately, Jack refrained from physical violence, but he did get him fired by telling the store owner he would never buy clothes from a store that employed a child rapist. It's unknown what transpired between the man and his wife after the verbal encounter since neither of them were seen or heard from again. Since the father had disappeared, and abortion was never an option, on Friday, November 14, 1958, a healthy eight pound-two-ounce baby boy was born to an unmarried, frightened, seventeen-year-old girl named Marilyn Cox at St. Joseph's Hospital in downtown Atlanta.

"Have you picked out a name?" the nurse asked as Marilyn was holding her newborn child for the first time.

"I have," Marilyn replied. "His name will be Anthony Dwayne. Dwayne is spelled D-W-A-Y-N-E," she quickly clarified.

"That's a lovely name," the nurse answered as she turned to leave the room. "We'll get that name added to the birth certificate."

As Marilyn looked at her newborn son wrapped in a light blue blanket resting peacefully in her arms, she said, "Did you hear that? Your name is going to be Anthony Dwayne. It has a nice ring to it, doesn't it? But that is not what I'm going to call you," Marilyn paused and touched his little nose and said, "I'm going to call you . . ."

"Marilyn!" Jack said loudly as he gave two hard knocks on the open door of her room, then stepped just inside the doorway and asked. "Are you decent?"

Startled by his abrupt entrance and loud voice, Marilyn checked her gown and adjusted her covers, then responded, "You're certainly in a good mood. Come on in."

Her excited brother walked up to the side of the bed, leaned over, and said, "Let me see that little booger!"

"Isn't he adorable?"

"He's a Cox alright. Look at that nose," Jack said enthusiastically and with meaning. "Have you given him a name yet?"

"I have. I just gave it to the nurse before you came in. His name is Anthony Dwayne, but I'm going to call him . . ."

Jack, being focused on his mission and formulating the right words to say to his sister, wasn't really listening, so he interrupted her by saying, "That's great, but what I really came here to do is make you a reasonable proposition. It's Friday, and I have to get back to work, so I don't have much time, so please hear me out, okay? I'm very serious."

Marilyn, stunned by the fast change in her brother's demeanor, looked confused, but then asked slowly, "O . . . k . . . what's your proposition?"

"As you know, me and Bonnie have two girls, and she can't have any more children, and you know I've always wanted a little boy to go fishing with, take hunting, and, well, do guy stuff with. Living in a house with three females just wasn't the way I expected to spend the rest of my life. And now that you're in this situation, I thought maybe you'd let me adopt your son. He already has our last name, and you can come visit him when you want. He'd stay in the family, would have the same grandparents, aunts, uncles, cousins, but he would just be . . . my son! I know I only have a third-grade education, but I'm making good money operating heavy equipment. Me and Bonnie aren't hurting for anything, and we would pay for everything, including your doctor bills, his medical expenses, and the adoption process. We would raise him as if Bonnie gave birth to him. We'd pay for his clothes, shoes, education, and even college if he wanted to go. He wouldn't want for anything. And most of all, he would be loved unconditionally by me and Bonnie, and Shelby and Jackie would play with him and help tend to him as he gets older. You could go on being a teenager without the embarrassment of being an unwed mother and without the burden and expense of raising him by yourself." Jack sat down on the edge of the bed, grabbed Marilyn's hand, looked at the baby, and then looked back at her and asked, "What do you say?"

The confused new mother shook her head as she said, "I . . . don't know what to say. This is definitely a surprise to me."

"Me and Bonnie have been talking about it for months. We just didn't want to mention adoption to you until we knew it was a boy. And now that you've had a boy, we're so excited and ready to move forward, that is, if you are."

"Wow Jack, that's something I'll have to think about."

Jack stood up and said, "Well, you think about it real hard. Raising a kid by yourself will not be easy. Mom and Dad are on board with the idea as well as other family I've talked to. It would be beneficial for both of us." Jack looked down at the baby, then cut his eyes at his sister and smiled, then said, "And for him too! Let me know as soon as you reach a decision. I'm sure it's a hard decision to make, but if you want what's best for him, you'll let us adopt him."

Jack turned to leave, then turned back and said, "One more thing. If you do decide to let us adopt him, I don't want you to ever let him know you're his birth mother; that's something you'll have to keep secret. You will be Aunt Marilyn to him, but I know you'll make a great aunt." Jack leaned over, kissed his distraught sister on the forehead, and said, "I love you." Then he turned and exited the room.

Marilyn didn't return his "I love you" as she had done many times. She sat silent, staring into infinity, and wondering what to do. She had only been a mother for a few hours, but is already facing an extreme life-changing decision for both her and her newborn baby. What was supposed to be a day of celebration and excitement had now turned into a day of dread and depression. She pushed the blanket back from her son's face, "Should I let my brother, who I love so much, adopt you? He can give you a life far greater than I'm capable of, at least at the moment. Or should I move forward with raising you by myself and trying to give you the life you deserve?" Marilyn laid her head back on her pillow, looked up, and said, "Oh God, what am I supposed to do?"

"Knock, knock!" Her mom's voice interrupted her thoughts. "Can we come in?"

"Certainly, Mom, Dad. Come on in."

As her mom and dad gathered around her bedside to see the baby, the words of her brother and his proposition faded into memory. *This is supposed to be a happy day for me,* she thought. *I'm not going to think about Jack . . . or his proposal right now.*

The voices of Tony's daughters harmonizing softly were resonating through the chapel as Tony sat silently listening to his cousin share the story of his illegitimate birth.

"Have you ever heard this story before, Tony?" Butch asked, knowing by the look on his distraught cousin's face that he had not.

Tony had been leaning forward with his elbows on his knees, and his hands folded under his chin as Butch was talking. He leaned back against the love seat, sighed, then responded, "No . . . no I haven't."

"Aunt Marilyn should have told you years ago. I'm sorry you had to hear it from me." Butch sat for a moment, waiting for his cousin's response.

Finally, he broke his silence. "See, I told you I was a mistake! Even Mom said so on the front porch of your house."

"She didn't say you were a mistake, she said she made a mistake . . . and she did. And she kept making mistakes, she just couldn't stop herself. She . . ." Butch stopped, suddenly realizing he may have said too much too fast.

Tony turned, looked at his now silent cousin, who had a strange look on his face, and said, "You were saying?"

"Well," Butch continued, "you may as well know the whole story, I didn't want to hit you with all this at once, but you may as well know everything."

Tony looked confused. "As if knowing my mom lied to me all these years and now hearing the whole story of how I was conceived out of wedlock isn't bad enough; you mean there is more?!"

"Well, sort of . . ." Butch paused. "It's more about your mom than you."

Tony looked at the coffin, took a deep breath, and let it out slowly as if he were bracing himself for what he was about to hear. He was not sure if he wanted to hear any more. What he had just heard shook him to the core, even though he had heard bits and pieces over the years. But realizing Butch was the only living relative he had left who could answer his questions, he knew he would have to listen, no matter how painful the answers were.

"Okay, tell me. I need to hear it if I'm ever going to have any peace."

"I agree. Once you see the whole picture, you'll understand you are not a mistake at all."

"Hmph!" Tony grunted skeptically. "We'll see."

Butch took a deep breath and began, "There's . . . another . . ."

Tony squinted his eyebrows and cut his eyes toward Butch and said, "What do you mean"?

"You have," Butch paused as he sighed, "a sister."

John Cox with his three youngest children, Alice, Buddy and Marilyn. (l-r)

Tony's uncle Jack who wanted to adopt him. Jack took Tony deer hunting a lot when he was older.

Tony with his 1st deer.

CHAPTER XVIII

WHERE'S MY BABY?

T he 1953 Ford pulled into the dirt drive in front of the Allens' house on Waters Road in South Atlanta. The young seventeen-year-old mother slowly exited the vehicle with her newborn son held tightly in her arms.

"Thanks for letting me stay with you and Artis for a while, at least until I can get on my feet." Marilyn shared her gratitude as she and her sister Betty walked toward the large screen porch. "With Mom and Dad working all the time, I don't know how I would manage at their house."

"You stay as long as you need to," Betty replied, staying close by her baby sister's side and holding gently to her arm as they navigated the rickety wooden steps leading up to the porch. "With four boys running around the house we won't even notice the new baby is around." Betty paused as she opened the front door. "Even though you have a baby now and are considered an adult, you do know Artis expects you to attend church and revival meetings with us as long as you're here, don't you?"

"Yeah, I know."

"That whole, 'living under my roof' thing," Betty chuckled.

"It's fine. I need to go to church; and besides, even though he is holiness, I enjoy his preaching, although I must admit he scares me sometimes."

"He's harmless! But I'll share a little secret with you . . . sometimes his preaching scares me too. I'm afraid he's going to have a heart attack!" They both laughed as they walked into the house.

"I think it's because we were raised Southern Baptist, and we're not used to all that hollering and shouting," Marilyn replied as they both sat down on the sofa in the small but quaint living room.

"I don't mind all the hollering and shouting as much as having to wear a dress or skirt all the time and not getting to fix my hair like I used to."

Marilyn was shocked to hear her sister opening up about her life as a holiness preacher's wife. She did not know her sister had not fully embraced her husband's teachings. She had always felt she was happy with her new religion and lifestyle.

"It is a lot different from the way we were raised, but it does seem a lot more spiritual," Marilyn injected.

"It is, but sometimes I feel . . ." Betty paused, "deprived."

"I understand," Marilyn said, agreeing, "I'm sure if my brother-in-law knew I was smoking again, he'd get on me."

"At least you waited till after the baby was born to start back," Betty continued. "He wouldn't say anything to you, but if he found out I was sneaking around smoking, he'd have a fit!"

"Betty!" Marilyn responded with eyes wide open. "You're not smoking again, are you?!"

"I'll never tell!" Her sister answered with a smirky grin. "I tried to quit several times, but it's just so hard. Artis has asked many people to pray for me to be delivered, but I can't seem to shake it. I quit for a little while, then I get aggravated at one of the boys or something, and I find myself lighting up again!"

Betty reached and retrieved her purse from off the floor, pulled a cigarette pack and a book of matches from deep inside, pulled out two cigarettes, lit them, and offered Marilyn one. After looking at her sister surprisingly for a moment, Marilyn took the cigarette from her hand.

Betty took a long draw, exhaled, and said, "I'm still trying to talk Artis into letting us get a television set, you know, for the boys, but he isn't budging." Betty looked at her baby sister admiringly for a moment as she watched her holding the unsmoked cigarette in one hand and stroking the face of her newborn son lightly with the index finger of her other hand. Then she decided to put her sister on notice that they might be moving.

"Did I tell you Artis put an offer in on a house in Union City?"

Marilyn looked up surprised and said, "No, you didn't."

"It's nothing fancy, but it's off a dirt road and out in the country. The house is old, but he's figurin' on building us a new house once we get settled in and all. He wants the boys to grow up with chickens and horses and be able to run and play in the woods."

Marilyn was staring out the living room window that looked over the porch in deep thought. Then she replied, "Wow, I wasn't expecting that."

"Nothing is final. That's probably why I haven't mentioned it. You and the baby are more than welcome to move with us, that is, if we wind up getting it. It'll be a little cramped to start with, but we can manage. If we can survive growing up with eleven of us in a small shotgun house, we can manage anything," Betty laughed.

"That's not what concerns me." Marilyn paused, then continued. "That's a long way away from my job, and I'm sure there isn't much going on in the one-horse town of Union City. How will I get to work? There are no busses running from Union City to Lakewood."

Betty had not thought about how Marilyn would get to work. She was just excited about the family moving to the country. Then before Betty could offer any response, Marilyn spoke up and said assuredly, "I can move in with Barbara and Rudolph. Barbara told me if I needed a place to stay closer to work, I could come live with them."

"Well then, problem solved. Barbara loves her baby sister just like I do, and she will take good care of you, probably better than me."

"I don't know about that," Marilyn smiled. "You and Artis have been very good to me . . ." Marilyn started to cry, then held back her tears and continued, "Through all of this."

Betty slid over and hugged her baby sister and held her for a minute, not really knowing what to say. Then she glanced at the clock, stood up, and said, "Oh my, never mind all that. We need to get ready for the revival meeting near downtown. Artis has his tent set up there. There's supposed to be a lot of people coming, mostly Black folks, so we need to get there early if we want a seat up front."

"Not those small, metal folding chairs!" Marilyn grimaced.

"I'm afraid so! Unless you would rather sit on a two-by-six flat board stretched across a couple of concrete blocks," Betty replied.

Marilyn rolled her eyes and said, "Pull up close. I think I'll just stay in the car!"

As Betty predicted, the tent was crowded with attendees who had turned out to hear the tall, slightly balding, gentle, redheaded preacher preach. Every wooden bench and rusty folding chair was filled, and dozens of people were standing outside the thirty-by-forty-feet open air tent with eyes fixated and ears listening as the loving yet fiery preacher warned them of the price of sin and the certain judgment to come.

As promised, Marilyn stayed in the car. To be respectful, she rolled the window down on the '53 Ford so she could enjoy the singing and listen to her brother-in-law preach. She knew he was going to ask her on the way home, "How did you like the sermon?" so she listened intently to every word. She was seated in the back seat with her newborn son lying in her lap, craving a cigarette, when her curious twelve-year-old nephew approached the car.

"Hi, Butch. Looks like the service is over."

"Yeah, we'll be heading home soon."

Marilyn noticed her young nephew wasn't being his jovial self, so she asked, "What's the matter? You look like you seen a ghost."

"No, it's nothing like that," Butch said as he twisted side to side with his shoulders drooped and his hands in the pockets of his overalls.

"Then what is it?"

"Well . . ." Butch continued. "I've been thinking."

"About what? You know you can talk to your Aunt Marilyn about any-thing. We've always been close."

"I know but . . . this is different."

"Well go ahead and tell me what's on your mind, Butch. You're too young to be keeping secrets."

"Well," Butch paused, partly because he was struggling for the right words and partly because he was embarrassed. "I know a little about the birds and the bees . . . I have three younger brothers, and we have animals . . . so I know that when . . . a woman has a baby . . ." Butch stopped again.

"Yes, go on." Marilyn smiled, knowing now what her curious nephew was about to ask her.

Butch continued, "I know . . . they have to have a husband. And . . . you have a baby and no husband . . . so . . . I don't understand how that's possible."

Marilyn, knowing the gravity of the situation and the seriousness of his question, began to think long and hard on how to answer him without making the situation worse.

"Well, Butch," she paused and looked away shamefully, not really knowing what to say, then replied, "instead of a husband . . . I had . . . a boyfriend."

Butch thought for a second, then asked seriously, "The man Uncle Jack was going to kill?"

"Yes . . . that man," Marilyn chuckled, then continued. "I want you to understand that I didn't want to have a baby without having a husband, but . . . when the man tried . . . I said 'No, please stop.' I resisted . . . but I was confused, so . . . ." Marilyn paused, looked at the curious face of the twelve-year-old, then hung her head and said, "I . . . let him."

Marilyn kept her head down and waited for a response from her nephew, but when none came, she slowly turned her head and, seeing the bewildered look on the boy's face asked, "Do you understand what I'm saying?"

Butch could tell his aunt was embarrassed, and she really did not want to talk about it, so he said, "I think so." Then he looked down at the baby and said cheerfully, "I'm just happy to have another boy around the house!" Then he turned and headed back toward the tent.

Marilyn sighed a sigh of relief as she watched her nephew disappear into the sparse crowd that was slowly filtering out from under the tent toward their respective nearby homes, many on foot and others toward their old, rusty, dilapidated cars and trucks. She laid her head back against the seat of the car, looked up toward heaven, and with tears streaming down her face, she began to pray, "Dear God, what am I going to do? I need your help, Lord . . . I need your help!"

Marilyn continued to live with Betty and Artis for a few more months until they were ready to move to their new home in Union City, at which time, Marilyn and her infant son went to live with her sister Barbara and her family in South Atlanta. Barbara had three children, Sandra who was six, Kenneth who was three, and Marty who was sixteen months. Barbara was a stay-at-home mom as well, so she agreed to help Marilyn raise her son and watch him while she worked if she agreed to help with a few groceries and household expenses.

"We don't have a house as big as Betty's," the five-foot-four, slightly overweight sister explained. "You'll have to sleep in Sandra's room. She has an extra twin bed in there. We'll have to keep the baby in our room since the bassinette won't fit in there with you and Sandra, but I'll take good care of him."

"Thanks, sis!" Marilyn said gleefully as she entered the first bedroom to the right off the short hallway in the three-bedroom, one-bath, 900-square-foot house. Marilyn laid her baby down on the twin bed near the window, then took her kaboodle and suitcase from her sister and set them on the foot of the twin bed closest to the door. "You don't know how much this means to me."

"Don't mention it," Barbara responded. "That's what family is for. I've already put Sandra's belongings into the two bottom drawers, so you have three for you and the baby. Dinner will be around 5:30 after Rudolph gets home. If you need anything before then, just let me know."

"I do need to feed the baby. Could you warm some milk up in this bottle for me?" Marilyn pulled a glass bottle from her kaboodle and handed it to her sister.

"Sure thing," Barbara said politely. "It's powdered milk, you know. We're po' folks around here," Barbara smiled. "All I have to do is mix the powder with warm water."

"That'll be fine," Marilyn responded. "He's had powdered milk before."

Barbara turned and headed for the kitchen. Marilyn picked up her son from off the bed and sat down for a minute to rest.

She looked at her six-month-old son, who was still sleeping, and said, "Barbara has a son a little older than you. His name is Marty. You two will have lots of fun together. Hopefully, you two will grow up together and be really close. I plan on staying here for a while at least until I can get us our own place. Maybe I can find me a Sugar Daddy who will adopt you, then you'll have a real daddy."

The frightened eighteen-year-old started to cry but then pulled herself together, stood up, sat her baby down on the bed, and began to unpack their meager belongings from her suitcase and kaboodle and place them in and on the solid wood-chested drawer she would be sharing with her eight-year-old niece. She then hung a few dress clothes on hangers and placed them into the small closet near the door of the ten-by-ten-foot bedroom.

"That didn't take long," she said aloud as she sat back down on the bed and began looking around the room. She thought about how she missed school, being with her parents, the family farm, and . . . her innocence.

I didn't realize how one event could change so much in life, Marilyn thought as the tears began swelling in her eyes. She looked at her son, who was still sleeping, and said in a whisper, "I'm happy I have you . . . but . . . I wish I had done it right! Having a baby by yourself is hard . . . but I plan on making it work . . . not only for me . . . but for you!" She picked her son up and wrapped her arms around him and began to weep uncontrollably. While sitting on the twin bed in her sister Barbara's small brick home on Blair Villa Drive in South Atlanta, the frightened yet determined eighteen-year-old made a commitment that she would do whatever it took to give her son the life he deserved, no matter what it cost her.

Living with Barbara and her family worked out well for both the young mother and her sister. The new mom was able to walk less than a quarter of a mile to the bus stop where she took the Atlanta City transit bus to and from the diner. She was also able to pay her sister a little money every week, which helped with household expenses. The extra money also provided the Mosley family with a little more disposable income for an occasional drive-in movie, a small toy or game for the kids, and a quick meal out at a fast-food restaurant, which often included ice cream cones for dessert, something Sandra, Kenneth. and Marty had not had much of.

When Marilyn had a day off, she would often ride the bus around Atlanta, looking for a better-paying job, but since she was only eighteen, had dropped out of school, had no labor skills, such as filing or typing, she was continually turned away often without even an interview.

After realizing her only option for income was going to be waitressing, she decided she would search for a waitressing job with a better company and future. The change of mindset paid off. After looking for only a short time, she landed a job inside a retail store known as Woolworths, located in the Lakewood Shopping Center on Stewart Avenue in South Atlanta, a division of the giant corporation known as JC Penney.

Even though her waitressing job was behind the lunch counter inside the small department store, Marilyn knew she could make a lot more tips than the diner based on the large volume of affluent customers who shopped there. When she clocked in on her first day, she was adorned in a white uniform, white shoes, and a dressy white apron that was far better quality than the diner.

After only a few weeks, Marilyn had medical insurance for her and her son, a retirement plan, paid vacations and other benefits, and a new sense of pride and accomplishment that she had never felt. Yes, it was just a wait-ressing job, but for the mixed-up, messed-up mother of a one-year-old little boy, she felt prouder than an Olympic athlete sporting a gold medal. The proud teenager was truly thankful for the new position and opportunity that had been presented to her, and she was eager to learn the Woolworths' way.

Living with a large family, tending to the demands of a one-year-old, and working five to six days a week, including most Saturdays, the exhausted teenager didn't have much of a social life, so when one of her regular male patrons asked her out on a date, Marilyn eagerly accepted. She kept the man's name private and didn't share any information about her new boyfriend to any of the family other than he was good-looking and treated her good. But as fate would have it, the mystery man and Marilyn engaged in unprotected sex, and when she came up pregnant the second time, mystery man was never heard from again.

"Dammit, Marilyn," Barbara screamed as she stood, looking down at her baby sister, who was sitting on her bed with her head down. "Didn't you learn your lesson the first time?! Being pregnant at sixteen is one thing, but getting pregnant twice in two years and by two different men . . . AHH . . . that's insane! I don't know what to think of you right now!"

Marilyn kept her head down, sobbing. "I don't know what got into me . . ." She paused, then continued, "He said if anything happened . . ."

"He would marry you, right?!" Barbara hatefully interrupted.

Marilyn wiped her eyes, looked up, and replied slowly, "Well . . . yes."

"That is the oldest trick in the book, Marilyn!" Barbara said, raising her voice higher than it was previously. "Men have been using that line to get into women's panties for years!" Barbara turned and pointed toward her son, who was sitting in the hallway playing, then continued in a hostile tone. "Look, Marilyn. LOOK! You already have one child from a man who smoothed-talked you into the back seat of a car! What did he do? Promise he'd marry you too?!"

Marilyn put her head back down and continued to cry as her sister kept berating her. Finally, Marilyn couldn't take her sister's painful words any longer. She looked up and screamed, "I WAS RAPED, OKAY?!"

Barbara stopped in midsentence, looking with disbelief at her red-faced sister. Marilyn put her head back down and then uttered much slower and in a lower tone, "I . . . was raped."

Barbara didn't know what to do or say, so she stood silent, in shock and disbelief.

Marilyn gained her composure, looked up at her son, then continued, "I tried to stop him . . . but he was too strong. I kept saying, 'No, no,' but . . . after several attempts to stop him . . . I knew it was useless . . . so . . . ." Marilyn put her head back down and said shamefully, "I just . . . let him. I didn't want to . . . but I didn't feel . . . like I had a choice." She put her hands over her face and began to weep uncontrollably and so violently that she was shaking the bed.

Barbara immediately sat down beside her, putting her arms around her, and said, "I didn't . . . we didn't . . . none of us knew." Barbara pulled her sister's head over and laid it on her shoulder and let her weep for a while. Finally, she asked Marilyn, "You are talking about the first time, correct?"

"Yes."

"Why did you keep that a secret? Why did you tell everyone it was consensual?"

Marilyn sat up, wiped her face with her apron that she still had on from work, and replied, "Because when I found out how old he was and since I was only sixteen, if I had told the truth, he would've went to jail, and I didn't want that."

"Well, the SOB deserved to go to jail, or worse, messing with young girls! He should've gone away for a long time."

"Plus," Marilyn continued, "if I had said that I was raped, as angry as Jack was, he may have gone to jail for killing him."

"You're right about that! Jack does have that Cox temper," Barbara chuckled. "You really did that man a favor by not telling the truth. I hope he appreciates it."

"If he doesn't," Marilyn added, "maybe his wife did . . . who knows?"

Both sat in silence for a moment, staring straight ahead but seeing nothing.

Marilyn started weeping again, then asked, "What am I going to do?"

"I don't know, but knowing the truth about the first pregnancy doesn't fix this situation one bit!" Barbara, realizing the seriousness of the moment, began to feel angry again. "You've really put yourself and the entire family in a difficult predicament. Getting pregnant one time out of wedlock is one thing, but getting knocked up twice, well . . ." Barbara paused, then continued, "puts you in the category of a whore. I'm afraid this situation won't turn out as pleasant as the first time."

Barbara stood up, took a deep breath, and sighed. As she started toward the door, she looked back at her sister, shook her head, and then walked out of the room. Marilyn grabbed some tissue from inside her purse, blew her nose, and began wiping her eyes. She could hear her sister dialing the phone. She sat quietly, listening to see who she was calling.

"Hey, Betty! Listen, I have some bad news."

Marilyn put her hand over her face as she listened to the one-sided conversation.

"Marilyn is pregnant again!"

"I can't believe it either."

"Well, I'm already raising one of her bastards! I'm certainly not going to raise another one."

"Hm, hm. She'll have to give one of them up for adoption. That's the only option I see, unless you and Artis want to raise one of them!"

"Maybe if it's a boy, Jack will adopt it."

Adoption . . . adoption? Marilyn thought as the conversation between her sisters faded in the background. *I don't want to give this baby up. What if it's a girl? I've always wanted a little girl.* Marilyn pulled her feet up onto the bed and laid down on her side. She looked at her son, who was still playing in the hallway near the door. She smiled as she thought about how terrible it was getting pregnant at such a young age, even though it was not her fault, but also how wonderful it was to have a little boy to love and who loved her back. She also thought about how hard her life had been with one baby, the difficulty of working relentlessly to provide for that baby, and how much of a burden she and her son had been on her sister and her family.

As she lay there pondering all these things, she placed her hand on her stomach and said to herself, "Maybe adoption is the best option for you. I certainly can't give you the life you deserve. I can't even take care of myself." Marilyn stopped crying for a moment, closed her eyes, and then whispered a prayer, "As long as it can go to a great home, Lord, as long as it goes to a great home! Please make sure it goes to a great home." Then she drifted off to sleep.

Eight months later, Marilyn gave birth to a healthy baby girl. Immediately after she was born, the nurses carried her out of the delivery room and placed her in the loving arms of an unknown couple who were anxiously awaiting in a nearby room.

When Marilyn returned to her room, she was surrounded by family, but all she could think about was her baby.

"They didn't even let me hold her," the heartbroken mother said to whoever would listen. "The nurses didn't even let me see her face." The family tried to console the hysterical nineteen-year-old with words like, "It's what's best for the baby, Marilyn, and you know it's for the best," or "Your baby is going to a magnificent home just like you prayed." There were other comforting phrases offered, but they did more to upset the young mother than comfort her.

No one knows how Marilyn found out the name of the couple who adopted her baby girl, but she did. She also found out what they named her and where they lived. Later in life, Marilyn would talk a lot about Susan to close family and friends and share her heartbroken story of how she was forced to give her up for adoption, holding back tears as she felt the agonizing pain of losing her all over again. She often wondered how she was doing, what she looked like, and she always had hope that one day, she would be able to meet her and tell her how sorry she was for having to give her up for adoption.

Tony's mom & her biological daughter Susan Denise. They finally met in 2017.

CHAPTER XIX

THE RESCUE STORY

"Did you know about Susan?" Butch asked.

Tony slowly nodded and replied, "Not until I was thirteen."

Butch sighed and said, "That's a relief! I was afraid finding out about her would be a huge bombshell."

"I tracked her down about a year ago. I knew Mom's condition was worsening, so I pressed her for more information before her Alzheimer's got too bad, and she finally gave me her full name and birthdate. I put that information in a person locator website, and I found a Susan Denise Black living in the Atlanta area. I pulled her Facebook page up, and when I saw her picture, I knew immediately she was my sister. She looks just like Mom."

"Really?" Butch asked, surprisingly.

Tony pulled out his cell phone and showed her picture to Butch.

"WOW! The resemblance is amazing. No doubt about it, that's your sister, all right."

"I just wish I had found her sooner. She'll be here tomorrow; too bad you're going back to Louisiana tonight."

Butch thought, then replied, "Hopefully, we can have that family reunion you've been trying to set up for umpteen years, and I'll get to meet her then."

"You two would get along just fine. She says what she means and means what she says."

"No filter, huh," Butch said laughingly. "Just like your mom!"

Tony smiled, then responded. "They did get to visit each other at Mom's apartment in Christian City last year. Mom just cried and cried."

"I'm sure she did. That must've been quite an emotional moment for both of them."

Tony didn't respond. He started thinking about the last time he visited his mom at her apartment. He turned his attention toward the chapel as he noticed that the music and singing had stopped, and the remaining few guests were engaged in quiet conversation with an occasional burst of laughter. Butch looked down at his watch and then added, "Too bad I won't be able to meet her on this trip."

"I'll get to working on that family reunion," Tony injected. "Although I don't think it will be held in Louisiana."

Butch was not listening to Tony. He was focused on all the points he had covered and trying to make sure he didn't miss anything. He finally replied, "Well, cuz, that's about all I know that you didn't know. You do know what happened after the birth of your sister, right?"

"Pretty much. Mom met Vic when I was three, and they got married, spent their honeymoon in Nashville, Tennessee, and he adopted me shortly after they returned to fix mine and Mom's reputation, and so I could carry on his last name and . . . here I am," Tony said with sarcasm, holding his arms straight out to the side, and then dropping them back down onto his lap.

"You know," Butch said with purpose in his voice. "There is one more thing I need to address before we end this conversation about you and your mom."

"Oh yeah?" Tony looked surprised, "What's that?"

"This idea that you were a mistake."

Tony rolled his eyes and said, "Okay, change my mind."

"I was there when your mom first announced she was pregnant, I was there when you were born, I was there when you were growing up, I was your Sunday school teacher, I went to visit you when you went to prison, I was there when you started coming to church after you were released from prison, I was there when you wrote your first gospel song, I was there witnessing the miracle of God giving you the talent to play the piano and the bass guitar in just a couple of hours, I was there when you announced you were called to preach, I was there when you were ordained, I was there when you preached your first sermon . . ."

Tony interrupted. "WHOA! You didn't have to bring up my first sermon, did you?" Tony said, laughing.

"I still remember it! It was something about . . . 'graduating,' wasn't it?"

Tony chuckled, then responded. "It was called, 'Graduation Day,' and it was the most frightening ten minutes of my adult life!"

"I'm sure it was," Butch smiled. That's why we always remember the first one!" Butch looked at Tony, lowered his voice, then asked seriously, "Do you remember who else was there to hear your first sermon?"

"Yep, Donnie!" Tony replied hastily. "We didn't even like each other then, but she came to hear me preach anyway."

Butch chuckled, "I'm sure she already had her sights set on you by then, whether you knew it or not."

"That's what she said after we started dating." Tony grinned a smirky grin, pulled on the sides of his sports coat, and replied, "When you got it, you got it!"

Butch laughed. "You know you got the better end of that deal!"

"I certainly did, and I don't deny it one bit."

Both cousins sat silent for a moment, listening as the singing started again in the chapel. Then Butch leaned back against the soft material of the plush love seat and continued. "Now tell me, who else do you remember who turned out to hear you preach that night, someone you were surprised to see?"

Tony thought for a moment, looked down at the floor, and replied, "Mom."

"Yes, she did! And she had not been inside a church in years. Other than weddings and funerals, she avoided church like a plague, but whenever things were going on in your life that involved you and your spiritual advancement, she was right there."

"Now that you mention it, she was at my ordination service as well. I have a picture of us standing in front of the pulpit and one by the piano.

She had on a flowery dress." Tony squinted his eyes at his concerned cousin for a minute and then asked, "Where are you going with this?"

"Stay with me a minute," Butch continued with excitement, "Now tell me what happened when you started your church at the radio station in Morrow?"

"A lot happened, but I guess to answer the question you're fishing for, Mom started coming."

"Exactly! Here is a woman who had not been faithful to church since she was a teenager. Sure, she went to church but never really committed to God. She and Vic attended the First Baptist Church in Atlanta, but even you know that didn't work out well."

"You're right about that! I would feel like I had a great time in Sunday school and church, and then on the way home, all Dad would do is cuss and talk about all the hypocrites. Talk about the pot calling the kettle black!" Tony shook his head. "It sucked the joy right out of my experience."

"I'm sure it did, but what I'm trying to get you to understand is, well, when your mom was young . . ." Butch was stumbling, looking for the right words to say what he was trying to without sounding hurtful or demeaning, then he continued, "Well, I don't know any other way to say this except . . . your mom was wild! She had a wild streak in her as a teenager. She was wild before she married your dad, and she became worse after she and your dad divorced. And after my dad was killed, my mom wasn't a godly influence for her anymore either," Butch sighed. "She went wild too."

"What is it with these Cox sisters after they divorce or become widowed," Tony said, shaking his head. "Even Alice went a little bit crazy after her and Jimmy G. divorced."

"I don't know," Butch continued. "But that lifestyle of drinking and carousing around has caused a lot of major issues for some of the children . . ." Butch paused, then followed with "That's all I'm going to say about that."

Butch didn't need to say anything else; point taken. Tony knew his cousin was referring to his four younger brothers, one of whom spent twenty years in a federal penitentiary, and another who is dead as a result of a drunk driving incident, another who drowned while trying to swim across a small lake after becoming intoxicated, and the saddest of all, his youngest brother who attempted suicide three times before finally succeeding by putting a high-powered rifle in his mouth and pulling the trigger, leaving his two young children fatherless and his wife a young widow.

Tony also thought of the fear, mental anguish, and poverty he endured because of his mother's insatiable lust, alcohol abuse, and lewd lifestyle. She would come home drunk and pass out for hours, bring strange men to the home, and sometimes leave him with them while she worked so she could return home and satisfy both of their lustful cravings again before sending them on their way or back to their wives. He thought of the constant moving, never having an established home, staying with relatives, and attending thirteen different schools, where he was always the outsider and never had time to make many friends.

In a brief moment, all those past feelings, fear, and anxiety began to resurface like a volcano becoming active and getting ready to erupt after many years of being dormant. But what scared the sixty-year-old the most was the thoughts of suicide he dealt with as a teenager and coming close to taking his own life, and how grateful he was today that he didn't follow through on those temptations, knowing he would have destroyed not only his own life, but also the lives of his children, grandchildren, and all their future generations.

Butch, seeing his cousin staring off in space, asked, "Are you okay?"

"Huh? Yeah . . . I'm good."

"As I was saying, your mom was wild, she partied at the Nugget on Stewart Avenue and other night clubs almost every weekend. She and my mom got arrested one night because your mom got caught driving drunk in Hapeville. She was constantly sleeping around with different men, including married men. By all accounts, from a spiritual standpoint, she was lost as a golf ball in kudzu and on her way to hell! And then suddenly . . . you went to prison."

"For something I didn't do, I might add," Tony said abruptly.

"Yeah, but you know as well as I do that being an accessory to a burglary is the same as being guilty of burglary, at least it used to be."

"I didn't even get out of my car!" Tony exclaimed. "It was in Fayette County, though, where the meanest judges were!" Tony thought for a moment, then continued, "Well the way I look at the entire situation is that I got away with enough meanness and didn't get caught. I figure I paid my debt to society for the things I didn't get caught doing, and we will just leave it at that!"

Butch smiled. "Thankfully, you did get arrested because after that is when you got saved!"

"I agree. It was the best thing that happened to me." Tony thought for a moment, then chuckled. "Did you know that you and Marty were the only two people other than Mom who came to see me when I was locked up in Fayette County?"

"I didn't know that."

"And you both came for two completely different reasons."

Butch looked confused. "I came to pray with you and help you turn your life around."

"Yeah, I know you did, and I appreciate it very much," Tony snickered, put his head down in embarrassment, and added, "But after you'd leave, Marty would ease up to the bars and slip me a bag of pot."

"YOU HAVE GOT TO BE KIDDING ME?!" Butch shook his head in shock. "Right there in the jail?! Under the guards' noses?!"

Tony, laughing at Butch's response, replied, "Yep! I made a pipe out of an empty soda can. I'd poke tiny holes through a foil gum wrapper and secure it in the pour spout, then I'd use a . . ."

"I DO NOT want to know how you made a pot pipe," Butch interrupted. "I just can't believe you didn't get caught!"

"It was a concern for sure, so I kept the bag hidden in the Bible you gave me. I figured no officer would ever look there."

"I didn't want to know that either!"

"I'd keep it there until after the last count, then I'd pull it out, and we'd pass it around. We were all surprised that the officers didn't smell it. Of course, we'd laugh it off by saying. 'What are they going to do, lock us up?'"

"Lord, have mercy," Butch said as he shook his head from side to side. Here I was trying to get you to heaven, and Marty was trying to send you to hell."

"I told you I was a heathen!" Tony laughed, but then realizing he had gotten off subject, said, "Go ahead. I just happened to remember that." Then Tony said seriously, "But I do want you to know that your prayers lasted a whole lot longer than the momentary highs I experienced. Your prayers and visiting me meant a lot."

"Now getting back to your mom, I want you to listen closely to what I'm about to tell you. I think you're going to be thrilled with what I'm fixing to say."

Tony sat up straight, folded his arms, and responded, "I'm all ears!"

"Now let's recap. You got in trouble, you went to prison, and you got saved. When you got out, you started going to church. You were later called to preach, evangelized full-time for over two years, started a church, and then . . . your mom started coming."

"I understand all that, but I'm still not following you. What does this have to do with me not being a mistake? I'm a bastard, I dealt drugs, I'm an ex-convict, I've failed as a father, I've . . . ."

"Hold on a minute, let me finish," Butch interrupted. "We all have failures, but you just need to hear me out. When your mom was pregnant with you, she could have aborted you, let Jack or strangers adopt you, kept her pregnancy a secret and drowned you after you were born, or a host of other terrible things, but she didn't, did she?"

Tony took a moment, then sighed before answering. "Believe me, I've thought about that a lot, especially when I see what young and even some older mothers are doing to their unborn and newborn babies these days. It's frightening to think about. I'm just glad my mom chose life, or I wouldn't be here today, nor any of my children or those wonderful grandchildren."

"That's so true," Butch agreed, then smiled. "Remember when you were little, I told you that you had a special calling on your life?"

"Yessir, I do."

"I didn't fully understand that calling until just a few years ago." Butch leaned back, sat up straight, and started rubbing his hands together, then continued. "When you started your church, and your mom started coming, I was so excited. No one had been able to reach that heathen for fifty years, not my dad, Brother Talmadge, not even me. But suddenly, she took an interest in your ministry, from a distance, but interest nonetheless. After you started your church, what happened?"

Tony thought for a moment and answered, "Well, after only a few services, she hit the altar and got saved."

"Exactly!" Butch said with excitement. "You had become her pastor, her shepherd. She became active in your church, attended Sunday school and even Sunday night and midweek services regularly, started serving the Lord with all her heart, quit smoking and drinking, and changed a host of other things in her life that she felt wasn't pleasing to God. She went from heathen to Christian, hellion to being truly born again. She made an amazing 180-degree turnaround while attending your church, which was a great miracle for someone who was that lost and that far out in sin."

"She did make a lot of changes after she got saved," Tony affirmed, "but we started seeing a change in her a few years earlier when we started evangelizing—a small change, but change nonetheless. She moved into our house on Irongate Blvd in Jonesboro and paid the note and the utilities for us so we would have a place to park our camper when we came home. She'd also pick up our mail at our PO box and send it to us at the addresses where we were staying, and a host of other things she would do for us to help us while we were on the field. But what I remember most, and what I believe had the most impact on her spiritually were the handwritten cards, pictures, and letters that Rachel, Leah, and Sam sent her. Mom received quite a few letters from the kids, and they were usually signed, 'We're praying for you, Grandma.' 'Jesus loves you, Grandma.' 'We love you, Grandma.'" Tony paused for a moment, cleared his throat, and continued, "I know that had to have a huge impact on her spiritually."

"I'm sure it did," Butch agreed eagerly.

"When I was going through her things, I found several of those letters the kids sent her folded neatly in a file cabinet. If I were a betting man, I'd bet you that some of those letters had tears on them." Tony looked at his cousin, who was grinning ear to ear, then said curiously, "Okay, we both agree she made a lot of changes and stayed faithful to God until she passed away, but I also know by that grin on your face that you're going somewhere with this, so, say on, cuz!"

"Don't you see, Tony?" Butch said with a quiver in his voice, tears forming in his eyes, and nearly shouting because he was so excited. "You were the one who led your momma to the Lord! You literally pulled her out of the fire as the book of Jude explains! Had she not 'made her mistake' when she was a teenager and had she not given birth to you and had you not had those wonderful children of yours, she would undoubtably be in hell right now! If she had given you up for adoption, aborted you, or drowned you, she would have destroyed the very person who was going to reach her with the gospel and show her the love of Christ and lead her to Jesus." Butch lowered his voice, then said, "Don't you see, Tony? She would have never gotten saved . . . had you not been born."

Tony, suddenly trying to process everything his cousin had just shared with him, did not know whether to shout, run, or break down and cry, so he just sat motionless, thinking, staring.

Butch, seeing that his cousin was in a mild state of shock from what he had just heard, continued, "You were no mistake, Tony. God used you for his perfect will to save one lost sheep who wouldn't listen to anyone else. He used you to help turn your mom from a child of lust to a child of God! You're not a loser. You're her rescuer, her disciple, and the one who led her to a life of redemption. What you thought was evil in your life, God was working it all, not only for your good . . . but the good of your mom, your children, grandchildren, and others. All those things you went through as a child, teenager, and young adult; all the fear, loneliness, brokenness, abandonment, and even prison; all the sacrifices on the evangelistic field that made you and your wife cry and worry, all of it drove you closer to God and ultimately . . . right into the center of His perfect will."

Butch, still noticing his younger cousin trying to come to grips with everything he had just shared, said, "Now I don't mean to belittle all the things you went through; you've had a hard life, but I do have to ask you this question." Butch leaned forward, looked Tony in the eye, and said, "Now that your mom is spending eternity in heaven with Jesus, Alice, Barbara, and her other loved ones, wasn't all the things you went through . . . worth it?"

Tony started to respond, but he could not get the words out. Tears started rushing down his cheeks and onto his sport coat. Then, with a crack in his voice, "Tha . . . that's . . . a . . . lot to ab . . . sorb . . . it truly . . . (sniffle) . . . is."

Butch stood up, put his hand on Tony's shoulder, and said, "I know, cuz. I know. But isn't it wonderful to know that God used you to save your mother? Not many people get to lay claim to that. I know you two were not close after the divorce, and you held . . ." Butch paused for a moment, "may still be holding hard feelings against her for the hell on earth she put you through, but you have to let all that go. You have to forgive her. She was a sinner doing what sinner people do, and you have to rejoice in the good news of Jesus Christ that you've preached for years, and that is, 'Jesus saves the vilest sinners' and 'He offers forgiveness to all who believe.' As ministers of the gospel, we must practice what we preach, so all I'm asking is," Butch lowered his voice and said slowly, "that you . . . forgive her."

Tony nodded as he wiped the tears from his face. "You're right, but there is one more person I have to forgive."

Butch asked, concerned, "And who might that be?"

"My dad." Tony sat up, cleared his throat, and said, "Just before me and Donnie married, she insisted that I invite him to the wedding and that we try and make amends. I hadn't talked to him since I was twelve, so I didn't even know if he would even talk to me, but I called him anyway and, to my surprise, he was glad to hear from me. I invited him to our wedding, and he came. He drove down from Smyrna and had a picture made with us after Rachel was born, and we even had dinner with him and his new family at their home in Smyrna.

"Not long after we reconnected, he had an episode with a blood clot that had formed in his leg. The doctors scheduled him for emergency surgery, so I went to visit him the day before his operation. It was a routine surgery, so I didn't think much about it being life-threatening. I had never talked to him about Jesus and never heard him pray except when he recited the Lord's Prayer at lodge meetings. When he mentioned God when I was young, it usually had a cuss word associated with it, if you know what I mean."

Butch didn't respond. He just kept listening intently as Tony spoke from his heart.

"When I was visiting with him, there was this strong unction to pray with him. There was also this fear of him and a voice telling me, 'He'll laugh at you if you ask him that.' Even though this battle was going on inside me, I knew I had to pray with him, so I asked him to pray with me, and he did. I was so happy he did. He showed emotions I had never witnessed in him before. I truly believe the Lord touched his heart in that hospital room. The next morning when he was going down to surgery, his wife told him to say a little prayer."

Tony started getting choked up, so he stopped, took a deep breath, then continued. "She told me he smiled at her and said, 'I already have,' then they took him to the operating room. An hour later, his wife called and told me he had died."

"What happened?"

"The blood clot the doctors were going in to retrieve broke free while he was being rolled to the operating room. It passed through his heart shortly after he was put to sleep . . . and it killed him."

Butch sat back down on the love seat beside Tony and whispered softly, "As I was saying, God has used you for his perfect will to lead your family and others to Christ. Everyone, and I do mean EVERYONE deserves forgiveness, Tony; you, me, your children, people who have wronged you . . . and yes . . . even Vic . . . and your mom."

As Butch was speaking, Tony began to weep uncontrollably, something he had not done in a long time. His weeping was loud enough that Donnie heard him from inside the chapel. She peaked around the bifold door and looked at her husband, who had his face in his hands, then she looked at Butch, who looked at her and whispered so she could read his lips, "He's good. He's going to be just fine." Donnie smiled, then disappeared back into the chapel.

After a few minutes passed, Tony grabbed his cousin around the neck and said, "Thank you! Thank you so much!"

"Look around you, cuz," Butch proceeded to speak one word at a time, slowly and precisely, "YOU . . . ARE . . . NOT . . . A . . . MISTAKE!"

Tony squeezed Butch one final time before the two released, then he nodded his head and said, "You may not realize it, but you changed my outlook on a lot of things tonight, both past and present. I know this experience will affect how I look at my family, my mom, Vic, my calling, other people, and . . . myself."

"That's the little Tony I remember," Butch said as he patted him on the back." As they both stood up to stretch, Butch looked down at Tony's stomach and said, "Although you're not very little anymore!"

Tony reached and grabbed a couple of more tissues as Donnie and the remaining guests slowly emerged from the chapel, talking and laughing, with Bryan right behind them.

"Visiting hours are about over," Bryan announced politely as he pulled the bifold doors together that separated the chapel from the viewing room.

Donnie walked up to Butch and her husband as others gathered around Marilyn's coffin for one final goodbye before leaving.

"It sounded like you two were having church in here a while ago," Donnie said happily.

"We were close to being raptured at one point," Butch replied with a big grin.

"We were definitely having good conversation," Tony responded as he wiped the remaining tears from his face.

Bryan walked by, wished everyone a good night and a safe trip home, then exited the double doors and headed toward the lobby to wait on everyone to exit so he could lock up.

"I guess I better be leaving," Butch said as he took a quick glance at his watch. "Glenda and Jeff are an hour behind us, so it won't be too late when I get home as long as the plane leaves on time." Butch looked at Tony and said, "You're going to be alright, cuz. You're going to be alright."

Tony grabbed his longtime mentor again, squeezed him tight, and said, "You don't know how much all this means to me!"

"It was all my pleasure!"

"We'll let you know where and when we set up the reunion. Hopefully we can see you again then," Donnie interjected.

"And if you guys are ever in south Louisiana, drop in, and I'll show you what fishing on the bayou is all about."

"You can take Tony fishing," Donnie said smiling. "You can take me to the best restaurants."

Butch replied with confidence, "That, you can certainly count on!" The tall, thin, handsome gentleman turned and headed toward the front entrance. He offered a polite smile and "Goodnight" to Bryan, who opened the door as he approached and returned the same. Tony and Donnie, now standing by the registry arm in arm, watched with admiration as the strong but tender preacher exited the building, then disappeared into the dark, rain-soaked parking lot.

"I love that man," Tony whispered as he stared at the door that was slowly closing.

"Me too," Donnie replied. She wrapped both her arms around her husband's arm, pulled herself closer, looked up at him, and asked, "Feel better?"

Tony, still looking toward the door, gave a few slow nods and then looked into the eyes of his wife of forty years and said, "I do. I feel a lot better."

"So, what are you going to do now?"

"Well," Tony responded cheerfully, "the first thing I'm going to do is step in here and see who's going to IHOP. I'm starved!" Donnie shook her head and laughed as the couple stepped back into the parlor. Upon seeing the still-opened casket in the adjoining room surrounded by his children and the few remaining guests, he stopped, wiped the smile off his face, and said softly, "Then . . . I'm going home and rewriting my eulogy."

Tony at seventeen-years-old just before going to prison.

Tony's mom and his grandmother Mattie Cox visiting him when he was in Alto prison in North Georgia. He served four months on a one-year sentence.

Just four months after being released from prison Tony is thriving. He is standing in front of his newly purchased 1969 Roadrunner.

Tony & his mom sitting at the piano at Bible Church of God in Union City just before his ordination service.

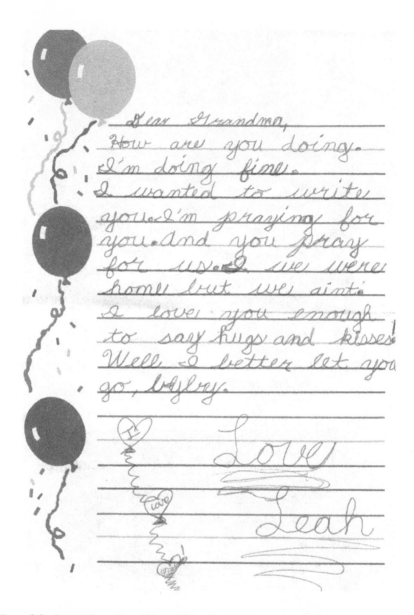

Dear Grandma,
How are you doing.
I'm doing fine.
I wanted to write
you. I'm praying for
you. And you pray
for us. I we were
home but we aint.
I love you enough
to say hugs and kisses!
Well I better let you
go, byby.

Love

Leah

One of the letters found in a file cabinet that Leah wrote to her grandma when her
dad was evangelizing.

CHAPTER XX

PROMISES KEPT

A light rain had fallen steadily all night and most of the morning, but it didn't dampen the spirits or stop the mourners from coming to pay their final respects to a woman they admired and loved. There were a couple of past coworkers who told Tony fascinating stories of her humor, love, and dedication to her job. Older family members shared funny stories and memories of when she was growing up, while many of the younger guests gave him consoling hugs and encouragement. Many close and distant family members had made it out for the 11:00 service. Bryan and several of his associates were busy directing traffic, parking cars, and making sure everything was in order for the family, attendees, and the deceased.

Donnie stepped into the hallway, looking for Sam and his family. She walked up to Tony, who was standing by the registry stand, and asked, "It's 11:05. Where is Sam?"

"He sent me a text and said he was close. I knew he'd be late if he went to LaGrange to buy that boat this morning," Tony responded anxiously as the couple walked toward the wide picturesque window and investigated the parking lot. "I told him he wouldn't have time to drive to LaGrange, take the boat back to his house in Henry County, and get here by 11:00, at least not in this rain, but he insisted on picking it up this morning."

Donnie could tell her husband was stressed, "You did let Bryan know, didn't you?"

"I did. He said it wasn't a problem."

"I'm sure it's not since they charge by the hour!" Donnie laughed as she tried to help her husband relax.

Tony kept watching the entrance through the light rain as he returned her witty remark with a smile. "He should have brought the boat back here. We may need to take it to the cemetery if we don't get this funeral over before the bottom falls out."

Just then, Sam's Durango pulled into the parking lot.

"There they are!" Donnie said with excitement.

"Yeah . . . but I was kind of hoping he was still towing the boat."

Tony's pastor, C. E. Popham, along with Tony's longtime close friend Jeff Crowe and his youngest daughter Brooke made the long journey in the heavy rain from the North Georgia town of Cartersville to pay their respects and show their support for Tony and his family.

Tony had heard Jeff sing an old song at church he really liked, so he asked Jeff to sing it after the eulogy, and Jeff agreed. Tony's biological sister Denise was also in attendance, and many of the family were excited to meet her for the first time. After everyone was seated and after the opening video had ended, Tony's children began to sing. Many hearts were touched as the family harmony resonated from the vented piano room that was located to the right of the pulpit. Tony was praying, checking his notes, and looking out over the congregation as the children delivered their heart-moving opening ensemble.

After they finished, Geoffrey Zimbleman, gave a brief but powerful message on God's grace and mercy. After he sat down Tony's son Sam, who does not sing often in public, delivered a heartfelt rendition of "Beulah Land," one of Marilyn's favorite songs.

Finally, it was Tony's turn to address the congregation. Even though Tony had taken on the role of "family preacher" after Butch left the state, and even though he had delivered several funeral sermons in front of many of the same people in attendance, he was still nervous. This funeral was different, the situation unique, and Tony did not want to mess this moment up. As he mounted the pulpit, he looked over the congregation and began.

"Today, we have all gathered here on this rainy day to lay to rest an amazing woman, a woman who did not use her past to make excuses for her life choices, a woman who endured abuse at a young age, a woman who had her hardships in life, a hard marriage, and like most of us, a lot of failure. She was a woman who was not perfect by any stretch of the imagination, but a woman who had come to know perfection through the shed blood of Jesus Christ, His marvelous grace and mercy and . . . His love and forgiveness.

"Many of you may know her as Delores. You may have known her as 'Sister,' 'Ms. Cox,' others here in attendance called her 'Aunt,' a few of you called her 'Grandma,' and others called her 'friend.'" Tony looked down at his notes, then looked back up and said, "but I am proud to announce . . ." Tony fought back tears for a moment, then continued, "That I have had the pleasure of knowing her as . . . Mom!"

The emotional preacher pulled a handkerchief from his back pocket, wiped his eyes, and then continued.

"I learned a lot about this amazing woman yesterday that I never knew, and I wish I had the time to share all the amazing things she went through to make a good life for me, my sisters, and others, but time would not allow it. But I do want everyone to know that we all need a lesson in judgment, mercy, forgiveness, and true faith. We also need to learn to treat everyone with respect and dignity whenever possible because we don't always know the entire story of a person's past or present situation."

For twenty minutes, Tony shared many other words of praises and admiration for his mother, their journey, and the miraculous love and saving grace of Jesus Christ. Many wept as he shared heartfelt stories of her transformation from a life of wickedness and sin into a life of joy, happiness, holiness, and love.

As he was nearing the end of his sermon, he asked Jeff to play softly and sing. As the melody and the words of, "Look What I Traded for a Mansion," began to echo through the chapel, hands that were once wiping tears were now being lifted in praises to God as tears of sorrow were being changed into tears of joy. As Jeff kept singing, Tony sat down, looked out over the congregation, and thought, *Now this is what a funeral of a child of God is all about!*

After the praises slowed down and the song had ended, Bryan peeked in the back door, and Tony nodded to him. Bryan came forward with two directors, turned toward the congregation, and motioned with both hands for everyone to stand as the other directors closed the lid of the coffin. The lead director then turned and motioned for Tony and Geoffrey to come down from the pulpit and take their respective place beside the now-closed casket, with Tony on one side and Geoffrey on the other. He then dismissed the pallbearers, which included, Tony's cousin Ricky House, Jeff Deleshaw, someone who thought a lot of Tony's mom and who is a close friend of Ricky, Tony's two sons, Sam and Caleb, Ginger's husband John Wallace, and Daniel Tuggle, who is married to Paula, the baby sister of Marty and Sandra.

After the pallbearers had quietly exited the chapel, the remaining two directors began to roll the casket containing the empty shell of Marilyn's lifeless body toward the now open double doors of the sanctuary, with Tony and Geoffrey side by side, following close behind.

As Tony wrestled with his own emotions, he could hear some of the family and close friends sobbing harder and louder as the body of his mom, now sealed shut inside the casket, passed by.

Once the casket had been rolled out of the chapel, Bryan announced, "The internment will be at Camp Memorial Cemetery just off Highway 85 here in Fayetteville."

Tony, now standing outside under the large overhang behind the hearse, watched as his mother was rolled out of the side door of the funeral home and placed behind the vehicle that would take her to her final resting place.

As Tony stared at the casket still covered by the spray of flowers, he thought about the specific instructions concerning her funeral that he found in the spiral notebook that his mother had written before her entire mind had surrendered to Alzheimer's.

"I want at least five gospel songs played at my funeral."

"I want to be buried in a pink or purple dress with a matching scarf."

"I want my long hair fixed really nice for everyone to see, and don't let anyone cut it."

"I want to be buried beside my sister Alice."

A smile came across the proud son's face as he realized he had checked off every one of his mom's requests except one.

"Why are you smiling?" The soft and pleasant voice of his wife penetrated the brain fog as she approached her husband, who was in deep thought.

"I was going over the list of all the things she wanted done when she died. I was checking the boxes."

Donnie grabbed her husband's hand, looked him in the eye, and replied, "You did great!"

"Well, thank you," Tony replied as he peeked out from under the pavilion and looked up at the sky. "Now if this rain will just stay drizzling like this a few more minutes, we won't get too wet at the graveside."

No sooner than Tony spoke those words, heavy rain began to fall.

"You spoke too soon," Donnie said, smiling.

"Yes, I did!" Tony rolled his eyes as he continued. "If Sam hadn't been late, we'd be under the tent finishing up right now! Why did he . . ." Tony stopped mid-sentence, looked at his wife, smiled, and then said sweetly, "I'm just glad he came. He's a great kid."

Donnie smiled back and replied sheepishly, "It looks like Butch really helped you last night."

Tony smiled, put his arm around Donnie and said in a softer tone, "He certainly did . . . he really did."

As family and friends exited the side door of the chapel with umbrellas in hand, many made their way to their vehicles that were pre-parked in a straight line behind the hearse while a few said their goodbyes to Tony and Donnie, then headed to their vehicles, choosing to skip the internment due to the heavy rain that had recently started falling. As the pallbearers loaded the body into the back of the long tan station wagon, Tony and Donnie walked to their truck that was parked directly behind the hearse and climbed in.

During the short two-mile drive from the funeral home to the cemetery, Tony's heart filled with gratitude as complete strangers pulled their vehicles to the side of the road to pay homage to a woman they didn't even know. As he admired their respectfulness, he thought, *If only they had known her, her difficult choices, her abuse, her . . . conversion.* Then he hit the steering wheel with both hands and cried out, "If only I HAD KNOWN HER, her difficult choices, her sacrifice!"

Tony looked at his wife, tears starting to flow down his face, then he continued in a broken and somber apologetic voice, "I would've treated her differently . . . If only I had known . . ." Tony looked at the back of the hearse and whispered, "I'm sorry. Momma. I'm sorry . . . I didn't know . . ."

Donnie didn't say a word. She just leaned closer and laid her hand on her grieving husband's shoulder and kept her other hand close to the steering wheel in case she needed to help him drive. Tony immediately suppressed his tears and emotions and regained his composure. He under-stood he needed to be in control of the vehicle and stay strong for the rest of the family. He dismissed his thoughts and focused on the hearse directly in front of him, keeping silent as the police escort with lights flashing led the procession through the heavy rain and slippery streets to the entrance of the cemetery.

As Tony followed the hearse into Camp Memorial Cemetery, he noticed a large tent over the grave site where his Uncle Bob and Aunt Alice had been laid to rest years earlier. Just as instructed, there was a six-foot-deep hole dug next to where Alice was buried. The rain was falling harder now and was wreaking havoc on the funeral home tent. As the remaining mourners exited their cars with umbrellas in hand, they stayed back as the pallbearers pulled the coffin from the rear of the hearse and carried it the one hundred or so feet across the rain-soaked grass and placed it on the straps of the lowering device that had been placed over the six-foot-deep hole.

Once the casket was in place, Bryan asked Tony, his sisters, and other immediate family to take their place under the tent in one of the metal folding chairs that was facing the grave. Bryan was not expecting the tent to be leaking, especially over where the family was to be seated, so before the family sat down, Bryan, his staff, and even some in attendance wiped off the seats with handkerchiefs, tissues, and other available cloth or paper items. As Tony and the rest of the family took their seat, some of the guests stood outside the tent, holding their umbrellas over the family, choosing rather to get soaked themselves than let the family get wet.

Caleb held his umbrella over his dad and mom since most of the rain was leaking through the tent above them. Tony encouraged him to come inside and take his seat with the rest of the family, but he refused and stood outside the tent, making sure his parents, especially his dad, stayed dry and could enjoy the final moments he had left on earth with his mom above ground.

Tony looked about him and seen a sight that truly blessed his heart. Sam had put his umbrella over his brother, someone had put their umbrella over Sam, someone then put their umbrella over that person, and all the way around the tent, the same scenario had presented itself with no one being left uncovered. As Tony looked around again at every one who had braved the rain to show their love and support for him and his mom, he thought, *People here truly are good people and have a caring heart, and the rain has brought the best out of everyone* . . . A smile came across his face as he whispered, "Including me."

Brother Z had agreed to give the graveside benediction, so after assessing the leaky tent situation, Tony asked him to keep it short, and he did.

After Brother Z finished praying, he began to shake hands with the family seated in the front row, which included Tony's Aunt Carol, his sisters, his daughters, and Donnie. As Brother Z made his way toward him, Tony looked up at the casket that was only a few feet away and whispered with a quivering voice, "I'm sorry . . . Momma." When Brother Z got to Tony, he stood up, gave him a big hug, and said, "Thank you very much. You did a fantastic job."

"Thank you for allowing me this great honor," Geoffrey responded. "Your mom was a great woman."

Tony sat back down as Geoffrey proceeded to shake hands until he had shaken hands with every mourner, including the wet ones. Bryan then stepped under the tent, gave a concerned apology for the leak, thanked everyone for their enduring patience, and dismissed the family. As Tony and Donnie stood up, Caleb handed them their umbrellas.

As they stepped out from under the tent, family and friends said their goodbyes as they hurried to their vehicles. John Kiker, one of Tony's longtime friends and favorite preachers, was also among the supporters. Being the jovial person he is, he came up to Tony and asked, "Where we goin' to eat. I know you bunch of StCyrs are goin' to eat som'weers."

Tony laughed and welcomed his longtime friend's sense of humor. He then replied, "Well, my sister Joyce had asked where a buffet was close by, so I think we are all going to Tim's here in Fayetteville.

"Sounds good to me," the short stocky fifty-something-year-old country preacher said in his frank Southern drawl, "I'm so hongery I could eat a horse."

Tony looked down at his pudgy friend and replied, "Looks like you ate a Clydesdale already!"

Both laughed, then the two shared a few memories about Tony's mom, Donnie's parents, Brother and Sister Stapp, his dad Marlin, and good times at the radio station church in Morrow. Then John shook Tony's hand and said, "I'll see you ov'r 'er at the buffet, but don't wait too long. You might not git'ney chicken!"

When everyone had finally left the area, Tony walked back under the tent. He stood at the head of the casket and broke two roses off the large spray, one red and one yellow. Donnie, who was talking to Terry and Beverly Waldrop, asked to be excused and then walked under the tent slowly to where her husband was standing now, holding the two roses up to his heart.

"You, okay?" his loving wife asked with a concerned voice of empathy.

"I think so. I just wish Mom had told me all the heartache and pain she went through for me. It would have really changed my opinion of her, the way I treated her, the way I thought of her . . . Why did she lie to me? Why didn't she . . . just tell me . . . the truth?!"

Tony began to cry again as he whispered, "I was so mean to her. I called her a whore, a . . . ." Tony could not continue. He just stood by his mom's casket, sobbing and sobbing.

Donnie motioned for everyone to just go on to the restaurant and give Tony some time. Beneath the noise of rain falling steadily upon the cloth tent, water dripping on a few metal folding chairs, the sounds of car doors opening and shutting, engines starting, and water being squeezed out from under moving tires under the weight of heavy vehicles on asphalt as the remaining mourners passed by exiting the cemetery, you could hear a passionate and heartbroken son weeping and apologizing to his mom.

Donnie didn't answer him. She just put both her arms around his left arm and pulled herself closer. After only a few minutes, Tony raised his head, wiped his face with the handkerchief he had used earlier, changed his demeanor, and said, "I'm okay now. I'm good."

Donnie pulled back, looking surprised. Tony, noticing the look of concern on her face, said, "None of those things matter now. None of it matters. Let's go eat."

Tony started to exit the tent when his wife, still holding onto his arm, pulled him back and said, "Whoa Tiger, what do you mean by 'none of it matters'?"

"Well, I'm here beside her empty shell, and she's in heaven. After Butch and I talked last night . . . well, I forgave her. I also forgave my dad and everyone else I felt had wronged me. I even forgave myself. I also forgave everyone who hurt you and the kids. And now, since Mom is with Jesus, I'm sure she's not holding any hard feelings toward me for what I said or how I treated her, so none of it matters because I'm forgiven too.

"Now I can't speak for Sam or Leah or anyone else for that matter, but I'm certain Mom forgave me even before she died because, over the past few years, as you know, she treated me more like her son than an inconvenience. I still have hurt because of the way I was treated, and I'll need time to heal, and I still have a lot of regret for the way I treated her and the things I said about her, even though they were done in ignorance, but I think I know how to make it up to her."

Donnie thought for a moment and then asked, confused, "How do you plan on doing that, honey? She's . . . gone."

"But her reputation isn't, and I need to fix that. I want to share her amazing life story and her marvelous testimony." Tony paused, then said proudly, "I'm going to write a book!"

Donnie smiled, knowing her husband had promised to author a few books in the past but never did, and knowing he had a lot of unfinished songs stuffed in a few drawers, answered with a tad of sarcasm, "O . . . k." She then pulled on her husband's arm as they opened their umbrellas and walked out from under the tent.

As they walked toward the truck, Donnie looked skyward and said, "Looks like the rain is letting up."

Tony, realizing there was a bit of sarcasm in his wife's voice, wasn't deterred. He began again, "I may call it, 'Marilyn' or 'Why Didn't She Tell Me' or 'From Rape to Redemption' or . . . who knows, but I'm going to write it. You just wait and see. I feel everyone needs to hear her amazing story, which is my story, and my dad's story, Denise's story, Joyce and Ginger's story, even our children and grandchildren's story. After all, none of them would be here if she had made the wrong choice at sixteen.

"Look at all the lives she saved by choosing life! I don't care if just our children and their children and the great grandchildren read it. I'm going to author a book. I can promise you that." Tony stopped, then asked his wife, "Don't you agree that a story like ours should be shared?"

"I agree, but let's go eat, there are a lot of people waiting on us at Tim's."

As the couple continued toward the truck, Tony sniffed the two roses he had cut from the spray, then turned to take one last look at the casket that was still seated on the lowering device over the open grave. He watched as the gravediggers walked up, made a few adjustments, then started lowering the casket into the wet muddy hole beside his Aunt Alice's grave.

A sense of pride and accomplishment mixed with sadness and relief came across the sixty-year-old as he observed his mother's casket being slowly lowered into her final resting place. The melancholy feelings brought both tears . . . and a smile.

"Check!"

Donnie smiled, knowing her husband had just completed the last remaining task on his mother's list.

Just before the casket disappeared, Tony whispered, "Au revoir maman, a demain."

Donnie looked at her husband and asked softly, "That was French, wasn't it?"

"Yes . . . yes it was."

"What did you say? It was so pretty."

An unexplainable peace came across the proud son as he replied, "'Au revoir, maman' means, 'Goodbye momma.'"

"And what does 'A demain' mean?"

Tony looked at his wife, then looked back at the now empty space where his mom's casket was just sitting, and replied, "See you again soon."

THE PAUSE

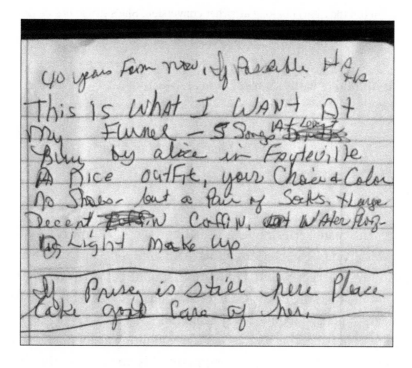

The handwritten note Tony found when he was moving his mom to his home. Her dog Prissy had already passed away.

Marilyn (on the right) not long after her conversion. She's seated beside Betty Morgan a dear sister from church.

The epitaph on the marker where Marilyn Cox StCyr has been laid to rest:

"From Child of Lust To Child of Love".

Follow Up

After the manuscript review, the editor sent me a message stating, "Some stories, though entertaining to read, don't appear to have a clear purpose in the larger work. The author should consider asking themselves, 'What does this story prove/communicate to readers?' and 'What are readers supposed to take away from this story?'"

I fully understood the editors' concerns. Putting a story about a whistling baby, a boy hitting his first homerun, his younger brother hitting his 1st grand slam, etc., in a book like this doesn't seem to fit the narrative of the books main story line. But I totally disagree. For you see dear reader, it doesn't take a rocket scientist to realize that if my mother and

202

grandparents had insisted on aborting me since she was only 16 years old "and had her whole life ahead of her" and since "she was a rape victim and shouldn't be forced to have me", then there would never have been a Whistling Baby, Gentle Giant, Turtle, Sweet Leah, or even a Tony, who became a preacher, led many souls to the Lord and was instrumental in helping rescue his mother from a life of wickedness and sin.

Elective abortion for any reason doesn't destroy just one life, but generations of lives, precious lives that would have been the offspring of the dead child and future adult. So, you bet I'm Pro-Life, and I make no apologies for it! Jesus said, "The thief cometh not, but for to steal, and to kill, and to destroy: I am come that **_they_** might have life, and that **_they_** might have it more abundantly," John 10:10. I am so glad that my mom and grandparents didn't let the "Thief" get me, and so are my children and grandchildren. And for the future generations that I will never know, I hope after you read this story you will appreciate the life altering, history changing decision a brave 16-year-old expectant mother made in 1958.

Thank you, mom.
Tony StCyr

Printed in the USA
CPSIA information can be obtained
at www.ICGtesting.com
LVHW042028050524
779411LV00020B/258/J